Seasons

A Woman's 6-Week Path to
Identity, Healing, and Purpose

TERI CRAFT • RACHEL CHANEY • DEBBIE RASA

 LIFE UNPLUGGED

www.livelifeunplugged.org

Seasons: A Woman's 6-Week Path to Identity, Healing, and Purpose
© 2022 Teri Craft, Rachel Chaney, and Debbie Rasa

CONTENTS

Introduction

We all have stories; and while the possibilities of how our unique adventures play out are endless, they all have something in common... Time. Not the *length* of time, rather, the reality of time's fingerprint interwoven into the rhythm of our story. That's the common thread that touches us all. The eternal echo of Ecclesiastes 3:18[1] and its poetic reminder that everything happens in God's timing. Seasons come, and seasons go. It is an inevitable truth. Yet, our stories weave through time like a red thread that gives validity to the One whose image we bear. **Our stories matter.**

Our individual stories, with all the ups and downs, are where we touch the tangible evidence of our potential to grow, change, and understand who we are and what we're called to do with the time we are given on earth. Often, we are encouraged to know and live out our lives embracing our truest identity in Christ, yet, for many, this is as elusive as the concept of time itself. For countless women, this chasm of understanding has caused a great deal of frustration, fear, and shame leaving many stagnate and hopeless.

1,A Time for Everything 1

3 For everything there is a season,
a time for every activity under heaven.
2 A time to be born and a time to die.
A time to plant and a time to harvest.
3 A time to kill and a time to heal.
A time to tear down and a time to build up.
4 A time to cry and a time to laugh.
A time to grieve and a time to dance.
5 A time to scatter stones and a time to gather stones.
A time to embrace and a time to turn away.
6 A time to search and a time to quit searching.
A time to keep and a time to throw away.
7 A time to tear and a time to mend.
A time to be quiet and a time to speak.
8 A time to love and a time to hate.
A time for war and a time for peace.

1 Ecclesiastes 3:1-8 (NLT)

This is your invitation to change that thought process and explore what it means to travel the dusty road of identity formation through life's seasons. What is the ultimate goal? To live and lead well. This concept and Four-Phase growth model called *Seasons,* is less about age, and more about how we, as women, traverse the innumerable times we are presented with growth opportunities when life presses in hard. These phases are potential scenarios that you, or someone you are leading, may identify with, and can be used as a fluid paradigm in your current and future seasons of life as an inspiration and guide. The truth is, we, as females, are imbued with the unique fingerprint of our Creator. This means that we have special ways of expressing our distinct qualities of beauty, emotion, and power. The question becomes, "How do we grow in these unique qualities through the ups and downs of our personal stories?"

We all understand the power of story in our unique perspectives for we bear the scars, not only of the pain that comes to all of us in one form or another through time, but also of the unimaginable power of redemption, redirection, and re-creation in and through Jesus. Each of us, as authors of this book, represent three different seasons of feminine experience.

I (Rachel) recently married the love of my life, Connor, in the season of COVID, a time in which my dream wedding was much different than I expected. We have no children yet, but are raising an energetic pup named Obi, and I am currently completing my Master's degree in Clinical Counseling. I moved from my lifelong home in California to begin a new life across the country on the coast of South Carolina. Quality Time is my love language, so you can imagine the fun adventures we go on, especially if it involves delicious food, hanging with friends, and country music!

I (Teri) currently reside with my husband, James, in California. We have a daughter (Rachel) who is married, a daughter in college, and a daughter in high school. I am an Associate Licensed Professional Counselor and the Co-Founder of Life Unplugged, an organization that exists to provide transformational opportunities to individuals and couples in need of enrichment or recovery. I have navigated the very difficult journey of marriage restoration and repair from betrayal, and consider it a blessing to advocate for others who find themselves in a similar tragedy. Walking alongside others is my calling; and my passions include worship, reading, music, long walks with James, and all things chocolate!

I (Debbie) currently live in the Dallas area, and have for many years, but I was born and raised in Des Moines, Iowa. I started working at a young age and have been in the corporate world most of my adult life. My husband and I lead a growing company, and I've been fortunate to have been a board member of both for-profit and non-profit organizations. I came to know the Lord late in life. Through my story (testimony), you will hear how I developed a passion for relationships and marriage. I love to fly and became a private jet pilot at the ripe old age of almost-50. I also enjoy skiing, biking, personal leadership development, self-awareness, and philanthropy. My deepest joy is experienced when spending time with my three adult daughters, their husbands, my six adorable grandchildren, and extended family and friends.

As you can see, we are a diverse group with numerous life experiences to share with you as you walk through this 6-week study. The growth model we will utilize throughout *Seasons* has emerged from many years of working with women in multiple settings, through reading and research, from real life experiences, and through the creative leading of Christ.

Real women's voices have shaped this narrative, illuminating a valid path toward growing in the beauty of a Christ-focused identity, and ultimately to leading others in the same endeavor. Our question is simply this:

> **What if we took the time to really understand how to navigate the specific seasons, or potential "phases," of our development in such a way that we, and other women around us, could be unleashed into our greatest potential in Christ?**

Each week, you will have an opportunity to dive into daily prompts that we pray will stretch and grow you in ways you never thought possible as you journey on your own personal path to beauty and identity based in Christ.

Will you take this adventure with us?

Week 1

Introduction

1. What areas are you hoping to grow in through this study? What do you feel curious about?

_____

_____

_____

_____

2. What are you most apprehensive about in terms of this study?

_____

_____

_____

_____

3. What emotions stirred inside of you when you read Ecclesiastes 3:1-8?

_____

_____

_____

4. Have you ever felt frustrated, stuck, or hopeless about who you are or what you're called to do? Describe your experience.

_____

_____

_____

5. How would it change your perspective of identity development as a woman to know you had a clear and unique path to guide your growth in this area? How would you live and lead differently?

_____

_____

_____

_____

6. Who will support you in this journey? (We suggest you reach out to this person and express your need for accountability and encouragement as you dive into this study and growth model.)

_____

_____

_____

Self-Care Challenge

Try to set aside 20-30 minutes each day to take a walk, listen to worship music, do some stretches or exercises, or sit quietly and relax. Note in your journal how incorporating these intentional moments of self-care are impacting you.

(Self-Care may be a word you are not familiar with. You might even be thinking, "Is it okay to think of myself in this way?" The answer is a resounding, YES! Scripture, as well as solid research, proves that when we set aside meaningful time to pull away from the busyness of life and take care of our "three-part person" – soul, body, and spirit – we live much healthier, joy-filled, productive lives!)

Leadership Connection

One of the hardest things in life for people to overcome is feeling unseen, unacknowledged, or unaccepted at the most fundamental level of their existence. As leaders, we must understand that those we are entrusted to walk alongside may need to have this basic connection point met before we share additional advice or teaching principles. Let's take it a little deeper. Do you feel seen, acknowledged, and accepted in your life? How does this impact the way you lead?

Why is Knowing Our Unique Identity Important?

Have you ever wondered, "Who am I, and where do I fit in this big old world?" If you are like us, that has probably happened more than once in your life. So, what anchors us through the changing seasons? The answer is...you guessed it, Jesus!

The simple truth is that our Savior and His Word hold us secure, and at the same time, release us into unlimited potential.

But if we're going to be honest, there have been many days, months, and even years that it was hard to comprehend our truest selves in Him. So, if our identity is the sum of all we know and believe about ourselves, then understanding this deeply within our hearts is foundational to everything that flows out of our lives.

You probably don't remember much about your early years of infanthood and childhood development, but the cues you were learning molded and shaped you in many ways. Our ability as humans to see our emotions reflected to us through our mother's or father's expressions helped us to find ourselves, and gave us the ability to attach and bond in relationships. It also created a place for us to discover and learn how to sense what was safe, and what felt unsafe. This developmental process continued through adolescence into our teen years as we became sponges, absorbing information about ourselves as we interacted moment by moment with our environment. These cues, and the character development we were exposed to, informed us not only about our beliefs concerning ourselves and others, but also how we ultimately view God and His Word.

One reality we all face as we travel through life is that, at some point in time, we will experience triumphs and trials.

Some of us may have even been the victims of abuse, neglect, and oppression, or may have suffered a traumatic experience. The support we received, or lack thereof, also informed our identity development by either supporting the truth of who Jesus says we are, or by the unfortunate delivery of mixed messages, a lie or wound created by someone else set against that truth.

I was once asked during a season of trials to describe who the real Teri Craft was before all of the circumstances I had weathered had wreaked havoc on my life. I still remember sitting there, breathing in and out in complete silence, unable to identify myself apart from the things I did, or used to do, before I had suffered such great loss. As bad as it felt to be that confused, there was a part of me that was curious enough to open my heart to what Jesus had been whispering to me, *about* me, for years, though I had been too busy running from the pain and the lies I believed about myself to listen. With the help of some really amazing people speaking into my life, I finally came to realize that I had been wounded in the areas in which I was most gifted. The places that I had felt most alive in my life were the specific locations and battleground targeted by the enemy for my destruction. This reinforced the lies I believed about myself until I was effectively just a human "doing" instead of the human "being" I was created to be.

I (Rachel) have gone through seasons where I had no idea who I was in Christ. Instead, I tried to look for my identity in sports, friends, or popularity. As a young adult in college, I would walk across campus wondering if anyone knew who I was as I longed for people's attention. If that failed to satisfy the ache in my soul, I would walk onto the track where I competed as an athlete and hope that maybe *that* would be my identity. I was reaching and grasping for something that was not real. The truth is, I was looking for me. At one point, I hit rock bottom and felt utterly alone, isolated, and afraid. I wondered, "Why do I feel so stuck?" The things I thought were stable in my life were slowly falling apart. I needed to come to the realization that nothing in this world could define who I was. Only God could do that. But I had to get honest first. For all the days I spent wondering what I was doing wrong, all I needed to do was turn to the One who created me in the first place. I understand deeply that many people my age walk around having no idea who they are or what they are called to do. They fling themselves into their studies, work, or unhealthy lifestyles and believe that is who they are. I get it. But honestly, things only started to change for me when I began to embrace my story. Life hasn't always been easy for me. I spent a good portion of my life in a glass house as a pastor's kid and experienced first-hand the devastation that betrayal and failure can have on a family. I struggled with self-worth most of my life, but have also seen miracle upon miracle of renewal and restoration in each of these areas. The key that unlocked the answer for me was when I opened my heart to acknowledge that both good and bad were part of my story – part of what molded and shaped me to be the person I am...as well as the woman I am becoming.

I (Debbie) was always taught to perform and be tough at the same time. I grew up believing that I needed to take care of myself, no one else was going to do it for me. I certainly didn't need a man in my life, and if I pulled myself up by my bootstraps and brushed myself off, that would show true strength and independence. What I didn't know was how to feel about myself, from who I really was to what I wanted, or even needed, and I certainly didn't know Jesus. You see, my biological father left when I was one year old, so my Father in Heaven was never on my radar. My mother only spoke in negative terms about my earthly father. So, for me, it was all about performing to be loved and accepted. I knew if I was a "good little girl" and did everything right, I would earn the love and approval I desperately yearned for.

I grew up in a broken home where the life plan modeled for me was: fall in love, get married; if it doesn't work out, get divorced. That is what every generation before me and around me had done. I thought it was as normal as graduating high school, moving out on your own, and going to work. Granted, I had a wonderful work ethic instilled in me, but the result of being work-focused led to relational dysfunction and a lack of healthy self-worth and identity. I once was asked to explain what intimacy meant to me and discovered that what I described was codependence and enabling at its best. I had a very unhealthy understanding of intimacy and what it could ultimately look like. My past life was messy, and I caused a lot of collateral damage throughout my years on this earth. On the other hand, I have also witnessed incredible beauty and growth as I've walked through a process of surrendering and becoming more authentic and honest. Ultimately, I found myself. The person God had loved all along.

The good news is that we are all able to experience ongoing growth and restoration, but to truly thrive, we must first understand from the inside out what our unique identities are in Christ. You see, Jesus loves every part of our feminine soul no matter what age we are or what our struggles have been. He cherishes the parts we have in good working order, as well as our broken places in need of His healing touch. What He offers us is the opportunity, *when we open our hearts in vulnerability*, to rewrite the segments of our stories that have been lost, stolen, or hijacked through seasons and time.

Why is knowing our unique identity important? Simply put, it's the foundation of how we view ourselves in relation to God and the world around us.

Knowing our unique identity gives us hope to weather the storms that come our way through the different seasons of our lives and connects us in healthy relationships and community. Identity strength is what forms the basis of our boundary structure, gives us courage to use our gifts, and keeps us grounded in authentic servanthood. Maybe that is why, when we are confused or wounded in our identity as we three women once were, our life as women can feel stagnate and hopeless.

Here is where we begin our journey through *Seasons*...

If knowing who we are in Christ is foundational to us thriving and leading well as women, then it is helpful to have a clear process to guide us as we walk through each season of growth and development. The opportunities you will have this week through the study prompts are meant to guide you toward gaining greater understanding regarding the underpinning of how and why you see and respond to life the way you do. This process is essentially just the beginning of the journey. The concepts, or potential scenarios, presented will help you to create a continual inventory of your life as you are faced with challenges and opportunities to grow. Our prayer is that it will posture you to dive into the growth model in an authentic and vulnerable way.

Self-Care Challenge

Continue to set aside 20-30 minutes each day to take a walk, listen to worship music, do some stretches or exercises, or sit quietly and relax. Is this becoming a habit? What, if any, resistance are you encountering as you begin to take care of yourself in a new way? Listen to what you sense yourself needing as you dive into some difficult areas of your past. Do you need some extra TLC, or maybe more emotional support from a safe person in your life?

Leadership Connection

Have you ever noticed that it's hard to authentically lead when you are struggling with your own identity in an area of your life? We challenge you to navigate your leadership influence in a way that allows you space to grow and discover who you are while responsibly leading others to do the same. If necessary, give yourself permission to pause and seek advice, counsel, or mentorship. Asking for help does not mean failure. Advice, wisdom, and counsel serve to direct you toward empowered living that ultimately increases your capacity to lead.

Seasons | Craft · Chaney · Rasa

Day 1

First Things First

"How blessed is God! And what a blessing he is! He's the Father of our Master, Jesus Christ, and takes us to the high places of blessing in him. Long before he laid down earth's foundations, he had us in mind, had settled on us as the focus of his love, to be made whole and holy by his love. Long, long ago he decided to adopt us into his family through Jesus Christ. (What pleasure he took in planning this!) He wanted us to enter into the celebration of his lavish gift-giving by the hand of his Beloved Son."

Ephesians 1:3-6 (MSG)

1. Before we can do anything significant for the Lord, we must first seek to understand our unique relationship with Him. After reading the verses above, what are you feeling? Why?

_____

_____

2. This passage of Scripture makes it crystal clear that we are the object of the Lord's thoughts and desires, as well as the focus of His love. Write down any other phrases from this passage that describe His intentions toward us.

_____

_____

3. One of the ways our identity in Christ is shaped is through our personal triumphs and trials. Do you agree? Why, or why not?

_____

_____

_____

_____

4. What personal triumphs and trials have shaped and impacted your journey?

_____

_____

_____

Have you ever thought about how the uniqueness of being a female is a gift from God? We carry with us a part of our Creator by way of His image. As females, we most often experience life through relationship and emotional connection, and beautifully touch our world through a heart of sensitivity, creativity, dependability, strength, and nurturing. There is also a part of our soul that can be complex and surprising, even to ourselves.

As women, we often live with fewer compartments than our male counterparts, meaning more often than not, everything in our lives is more visible to us. This special fingerprint of femininity, if not understood, can sometimes feel overwhelming, damaging, or confusing. Have you ever heard the saying, "If mamma ain't happy, nobody's happy?" Case in point. Our unique qualities given to us by God can also be the very ground on which we experience pain and difficulties, as well as our greatest joys.

I (Debbie) believe, at times, we can all have an identity crisis of sorts, and we can become confused. To be honest, thinking about Jesus having my unique identity in mind before He laid

the foundations of the earth is difficult to fathom and perceive, even hard to believe. When I was growing up, my expression of femininity (physical or emotional) was often silenced. Perhaps this anecdote will adequately describe this phenomenon of conflict and/or confusion that some of us face as we grow through seasons of life as women.

Michael and I were honored to be highlighted a few years ago in the first chapter of a book called *Bigger Than Business: Real-World Stories Of Business Owners Living Their Purpose* by Jeff Holler. This is a small excerpt describing how I felt:

> Debbie also came to believe that she should bury her feelings and just keep working hard and pushing forward. She was often told to "dry it up" because there was no reason to cry. 'I was taught to pick myself up by my bootstraps, brush myself off, and plow through difficult situations without dwelling on them or dealing with emotions like fear, anger, pain, or sadness,' Debbie said. Still, Debbie was a sweet and kind girl, and a tiny mustard seed of faith was planted in her life starting at age 12. For two years, she and her best friend Kay went together to Sunday school and church. Debbie doesn't recall how she started going to church, but she does remember Mel, her Sunday school teacher who she says was 'a wonderful man of God, who...in retrospect, was like Jesus in the flesh to me. He made a profound impact on both of us, and when he died shortly thereafter, my faith seemingly died with him.'

Although Mel made it easy for me to start believing I am who God's truth says I am in Ephesians 1:3-6, it also birthed the beginning of confusion in my heart about how I am made uniquely feminine, and that God truly loves me exactly as He made me. Feeling that the people I loved consistently died or deserted me, I started to subconsciously build an impenetrable wall of protection around my heart and made a vow never to hurt or feel such unbearable pain or sadness again.

1. Review the passage in Ephesians 1:3-6. As you read it again, be mindful of how your unique life story as a female has impacted the way you hear and respond to the intentions of your heavenly Father toward you. What are you discovering?

_____

_____

_____

$2.$ Make a list of at least 5 ways you have witnessed the Lord demonstrating to you that you are an object of His love. *If this is hard on your own, invite a trust family member or friend to do this exercise together.*

*

_____

_____

*

_____

_____

*

_____

_____

*

_____

_____

*

_____

_____

The Search for Blessing

Read Genesis 27: 1-40.

My husband and I (Teri) have had the privilege of spending time with John Trent, Ph.D., who co-authored a wonderful new edition of the book, *The Blessing: Giving the Gift of Unconditional Love and Acceptance.*[2] In *The Blessing*, the concept of giving and receiving a parental blessing is beautifully portrayed. John expressed that one of the reasons it meant so much to him was that he, as with many people, feel as if Esau's cry for a missed blessing echoed his own as a developing child. Has someone in your life expressed this view? Have you ever experienced it? Felt like something was lost or stolen from you, and you were left sad and confused?

You see, all of us long for love and acceptance, for someone to really see us and validate our uniqueness as well as our pain. Some women have been the beneficiaries of healthy expressions of love and acceptance. If that is the case for you, then today's exploration will serve as an inspiration to do the same with your loved ones and the next generation. To give another the gift of a blessing. There is also a perspective that many women share that includes the reality that these needs have been unfulfilled, and for some, were tragically and violently ripped from them. Our prayer is that you will open your heart to explore how these experiences have impacted you, and how you can begin a healing journey from them.

1. Reflecting on Genesis 27:1-40, to what person, or persons, in the story do you most relate? Explain

_____

_____

---

2. Dr. John Trent, Ph.D., Gary Smalley, and Kari Trent Stageberg, *The Blessing: Giving the Gift of Unconditional Love and Acceptance,* Thomas Nelson (2019).

2. How does this perspective speak of your personal journey?

.

_____

_____

3. Something that is helpful to note, is that most parents are doing the best they can with the tools they have been given from their life experiences. Growth, however, begins in our lives when we are able to:

- *Acknowledge our unique or difficult experiences.*
- *Recognize if shame and fear have been a part of our perspective.*
- *Decide to open our hearts to a new journey with Christ as He illuminates our true identity in Him.*
- *Ask for help and support from safe people.*

Of the opportunities listed above, which do you find most challenging? Take some time to contemplate why you feel that way and explain below.

_____

_____

4. John 3:1 states, *"See how very much our Father loves us, for he calls us his children, and that is what we are!"* (NLT) The truth is that, no matter how our story reads on paper, we are loved and accepted by God and adopted into His family. How does this make you feel? How does your perspective change the way you see others?

_____

_____

_____

5. Can you recall a time you felt as if a blessing was lost or stolen from you? Explain.

_____

_____

_____

_____

6. Take a moment and re-read Ephesians 1:3-6 from yesterday's prompt. Let the truth of this passage bring comfort and encouragement to your journey. Take some time to close your eyes, quiet your thoughts, and breathe deeply, focusing on the words of this passage. What truth found in this passage is most important for you to hear right now? Write it here.

_____

_____

_____

_____

Note: As you navigate these prompts, you may discover that some of the memories that emerge may feel overwhelming. We encourage you to reach out to a safe accountability partner and/or counselor, as we have done on our journeys, to help you discover a greater degree of healing for the parts of your story that feel confusing, unsettling, or traumatic.

Day 3

A Glance in the Rearview Mirror

In the last few days, we have asked you to contemplate how your unique story has impacted the way you view yourself in relation to God, His Word, and relationships you've experienced along the way. Today's prompts will give you an opportunity to gaze a little more intensely into the rearview mirror of your life story with the hope that together we can uncover any burdens or lies that may have been passed along to you, were a product of your own decisions, or unknowingly attached themselves to you.

In our journey of feminine identity, it is essential that we begin to embrace our unique story, even if it has taken us on some very bumpy roads. It is in this posturing that we allow God to open our eyes to the catalytic ways He is growing and developing us into our truest self in Him.

The truth is, we have been strategically wounded in our areas of giftedness so that we would not reach our potential in Christ.

Think about that for a moment. One of the ways the enemy seeks to destroy us is in the area of our greatest gifting, in our most meaningful opportunity to connect with God and others. The problem is, most of us have had a great deal of this wounding in our early development, so it is either forgotten, shoved under the rug, or the memories have shame wrapped around them and we are afraid to deal with them.

One of the ways I (Teri) was able to find the places of my identity that had been lost or forgotten in the pain of my life story, was to take some time to create a timeline of personal tragedies, trials, and traumas. Now, I know this doesn't sound very appealing, but I can attest that it was very impactful for me and continues to be for the many women I lead through recovery and personal growth to this day. The easiest way to do this is to take a piece of paper, or use your journal, and split your current age into four segments. Each quarter will represent a *season* of sorts. In each *season*, write down any tragedies, trials, traumas, or impacting situations that may have affected you to any degree. Next to the tragedy, trial, trauma, or situation, write down what lie or perception you believed as a result of it. This can be an intense exercise, so we encourage you to take some time in prayer before the Lord to allow Him to prepare your heart for what He wants to reveal to you. We also encourage you to bring someone close to you along on your journey of illuminating these past situations. Whenever we are in a growth process, we need healthy connection and accountability.

Here are some examples:

9-years-old – I was repeatedly bullied by a neighborhood girl who told me I was stupid and not worth anything.	**Lie I believed** – Something is wrong with me. No one wants to be my friend.
12-years-old – My father abandoned our family, and my mom was left to raise my brother and me.	**Lie I believed** – Men cannot be Trusted. I'm not good enough. I can't depend on anyone.
25-years-old – I was diagnosed with a chronic health issue, but not healed.	**Lie I believed** – I don't have enough faith. I must be bad. God loves others more than He loves me.

Once you have your four seasons of tragedies, trials, traumas and lies completed, take a few moments to review the lies you have possibly taken up as part of your overall outlook and identity through the years. Are you seeing any similarities? Is this confirming some of the places you've felt frustrated and stuck but couldn't quite figure out why? (Remember that females often experience facets of their identity growth through relationships and emotional connection.) These lies are the places the Lord wants to redefine and restore so you can live in freedom and vitality as a woman of God!

Here is an excerpt from a book my husband, James, and I wrote about our season of recovery in life and marriage called, *EXPOSED: A Journey of Renewal and Hope.*[3] In this excerpt, you will hear how I felt about going through the process of looking in my own rearview mirror.

> What I uncovered was no less than the most precious and priceless treasure I could have ever been gifted or discovered. It was like I was sitting with my Daddy God, holding the photo album of my life. Together, we reviewed each and every picture, good and bad; He carefully and masterfully revealed the enemy's plan and then covered it with His grace and love, until my scars were no longer bleeding. The memories were seen through the cross, and my potential in Him began to unfold in an orchestration so sweet and loud, that no fear or pain could subdue its melody.

This heartfelt expression came out of the gut-wrenching exploration of looking back at the places where I had been wounded. The real truth is that when I had taken an inventory of these life trials, I noticed, as I got quiet and honest, that some wounds were still bleeding. Many of the lies I believed

3. James Craft and Teri Craft, *EXPOSED: A Journey of Renewal and Hope*, Pure Desire Ministries International, Gresham, Oregon (2020).

for years were in need of Jesus' healing touch, but I was too afraid and ashamed to go there. When I did, a treasure trove of healing potential leapt right back at me. And I can say without a doubt, the Lord was faithful to meet me right where I was and give me courage to continue in my journey of discovery.

Lord of all creation, we pray you will bring your healing touch to my sister, (say your name) as she courageously glances back in order to move forward. Reveal what has been taken up as a lie about herself that You never intended, and replace it with Your loving truth formed and fashioned just for her.

Day 4
Rebound

Read Mark 5: 21-34

I (Rachel) was a Division 1 collegiate track and field athlete specializing in the pole vault. Yes, that's the sport that involves running as fast as you can with a 13-foot pole in your hand and hurling yourself upside down over a bar way, way up in the air. Falling is something I know a lot about. I also know what it means to soar through the air, thirteen feet above the ground, and feel the elation of winning first place. Just like my experience as a pole vaulter, we all face the reality of having ups and downs in life.

But we are not alone. Everyone feels that way at one point or another. There have been so many times in my athletic career that I stood at the end of the vault runway staring at the bar 85 feet in front of me, thinking about the fall I had just taken and the pain I felt in my body, and just wanting to run away.

The concept of the word *rebound* has to do with the ability to spring back from force or impact. To rebound is to recover or to act with resilience. The most common use of the word describes what happens in basketball when the ball in play misses its intended goal and bounces off the backboard and back into play. This is the *point of new potential.* This is what we are given strength to do when we follow the path of discipleship. We allow God to bring growth and healing as we open our hearts in the good times, as well as the bad.

1. What does it mean to you to 'get up' after a fall? What gave the woman in Mark 5 the courage to press into the crowd to get to Jesus after she had suffered with no answers for so long?

_____

_____

_____

2. When have you felt as if you had nothing to lose, when there was nothing more important to you than what Jesus was doing in your life? If you haven't had that experience, what do you sense has become more important?

_____

_____

_____

3. Yesterday, you took time to review the difficult parts of your story and open your heart up to the possibility of finding lies or false aspects of your identity that have been a part of your perspective. That process is a big deal and takes a great amount of courage. Well done! Today, you are continuing your journey to open up a wider view of your life that has taken you through seasons of triumphs and trials. Will you give yourself permission to receive grace as you navigate your way, much like the woman in Mark 5, toward healing and your future potential in Christ? Write your thoughts here.

_____

_____

_____

4. Can you relate to any aspect of this woman's story? Write what you are feeling in this present moment below.

_____

_____

_____

When we begin to uncover the ways our tragedies, trials, and traumas have impacted us, it can feel discouraging. But what if we allowed ourselves, as women, to get curious about how God is using our stories to grow us?

5. How have you grown through your seasons of trials and triumphs?

_____

_____

_____

_____

_____

_____

Sometimes we learn to adapt to our areas of wounding when what God really desires is for us to go beyond adapting into *Resilience*. Resilience is best described as "getting up once more than we are knocked down."

People who are resilient have the ability to:

- Flourish under expected and unexpected change.
- Cope in healthy ways when under stress.
- Thrive in strong self-concepts.
- Maintain quality relationships.
- Integrate the good and bad in life.[4]

---

4. Geri Miller, Learning the Language of Addiction Counseling 5th Edition, Wiley & Sons (202

6. Which of the above statements seem easy for you? Which ones are more difficult?

_____

_____

_____

_____

_____

_____

Can I take a moment and encourage you? As I mentioned above, I know a thing or two about falling. I've experienced it over and over in my athletic career, but I have also experienced it in my life and relationships. I've had people walk all over me because they didn't think I was strong enough to fight back. There was a period in my life when I honestly did not know who I was or what I was supposed to do with my future. Because of that, I tried to find my identity in everything but what was real, reaching for something that wasn't even there. I started to feel like I had fallen too far, and not even God could get me to my feet again. But something changed when I took a step back and realized that my identity could not be found in the places where I was searching. I began to see that I was strong and courageous, and God did have a plan for my life. With the help of my family and some good counsel, I learned to integrate the good and the bad so I could live a better, fulfilled life. And just like a basketball that hits the backboard and misses the first hundred times, I found strength to rebound into new and exciting places of potential.

Day 5

Courage to Forge Ahead

Manifesto of the Brave and Brokenhearted[5]
by Brené Brown

There is no greater threat to the critics and cynics and fearmongers
than those of us who are willing to fall because we have learned how to rise.
With skinned knees and bruised hearts; we choose owning our stories of struggle,
over hiding, over hustling, over pretending.
When we deny our stories, they define us. When we run from struggle, we are never free.
So we turn toward truth and look it in the eye.
We will not be characters in our stories. Not villains, not victims, not even heroes.
We are the authors of our lives. We write our own daring endings.
We craft love from heartbreak, compassion from shame,
grace from disappointment, courage from failure.
Showing up is our power. Story is our way home. Truth is our song.
We are the brave and brokenhearted.
We are rising strong.

1. After reading this manifesto written by Brené Brown, what do you feel?

_____

_____

_____

5. Brené Brown, Ph.D., *Rising Strong: How the Ability to Reset Transforms the Way We Live, Love, Parent, and Lead* (2018).

2. Take some time to reflect on the process you have navigated this week. What have you discovered about yourself?

_____

_____

_____

3. What have you discovered about your perceptions prior to these activities?

_____

_____

_____

4. What will you need to forge ahead in this process?

_____

_____

_____

5. We encourage you to let someone know what you need in terms of support and prayer as you take the next steps in this study. **Write the name, or names, of people who will commit to supporting you.**

_____

_____

We are about to embark on the exploration into the *Seasons* Growth Model for the next four weeks. This process model was constructed and refined by bringing together what we have learned from our personal stories of identity development, years of experience in working with women in numerous capacities, reading and investigation, and the creative leading of Christ.

It is important to note that you will, at different times of your life, process through the different phases based upon new situations and circumstances. You will have the opportunity to use your newfound skills to traverse and launch into deeper levels of Balance and Advocacy as you gain awareness and resilience. It is also possible that you could find yourself in an earlier phase of your present situation if stressors are greater than your capacity or support structure can sustain. The "phasing" ability is primarily determined by your curiosity, willingness, optimism, accountability and vulnerability.

The key word for you to embrace, as you begin to examine and self-assess aspects of the Seasons Growth Model in relation to your own life, is *grace*.

We all need a lot of grace! Sometimes we forget that the capacity to which we are able to give grace is directly proportional to our openness to receive it. There is no wrong answer here. There is no shame or judgement in being honest with where we are on our journey of feminine growth and development. The truth is that we cycle through these concepts much like we traverse the seasons of time. Life is ever changing, so we have to get real with what we are feeling, experiencing, and perceiving if we want to be women who are "rising strong."

Ultimately, this development is as much about leadership as it is about our personal lives. Our goal as women of God should be to live and love authentically and with vitality, but to also tangibly represent the words of the great commandment; to love and serve others as we love and have grace for ourselves.

An important note: Some of the memories that may have surfaced from these prompts could contain abuse, trauma or victimization. Please hear our hearts when we take this moment to acknowledge your pain and the significance these events have had upon your life. We encourage you to seek help if needed in the form of trauma therapy, coaching, or counseling if you are feeling overwhelmed.

Static

Transition

Balance

Advocacy

Week 3

Static Introduction

We start our journey of the *Seasons* Four-Phase Growth Model with Static. As we mentioned previously, this journey is not about success or failure. It is about vulnerability and growth potential. We gathered information from interviews, poured through research, did some investigating, and took inventory of our own journeys through identity formation; and what we came up with are realistic scenarios, not shame-based accusations or judgmental verbiage. It's simply an opportunity for anyone willing to take a closer look at their present reality, have the chance to understand how some of their present perceptions might have come from past experiences, and then make an informed choice for each step forward as they move toward a future filled with vision and potential.

To be candid, I (Teri) spent the greater portion of my adult life in the Static Phase of feminine development. Yes, I had grown in a few of the areas past this initial phase, but for the most part, I operated internally from the scenario of this phase. If I can be even more candid, I can look back now and see that though I acted on the outside as if I had developed past Balance and into Advocacy in many areas of ministry leadership, I was hemorrhaging from the inside out, trying so hard to keep it all together.

You see, I thought if I was honest about my fears and insecurities, I would be a failure; and based on the lies I believed about myself, that was not an option. Not if I wanted to feel loved and accepted.

I (Rachel) have always been a careful observer. I watched my mom carry burdens that weren't her own, yet I didn't have the understanding as a child to comprehend how it was impacting her life, and how, outwardly, it would touch my own. I saw her as someone who would keep to herself and not necessarily stand up for what she believed. I learned that it was normal to let people talk down to you and not speak up. I related to the Static Phase for most of my development as a girl and young woman because I was in relationships or situations where I was seen as weak because I wouldn't stand my ground. People would walk right over me. I saw and knew that something was wrong but did not know how to take the next step. I sat back and let myself get hurt because I did not know, or have the knowledge, to really become my true self in Jesus. I saw myself as someone that wasn't worthy of having a voice. I was essentially stuck in this Static place, uncomfortable in it, yet too afraid to make a change.

Something happened when I saw my mom take steps of faith forward in her journey. It was a slow and steady process. I watched her learn how to accept who she was, and is, in Christ, and allow her heart to have compassion for her story. It gave me courage to see her live with healthy boundaries and use her voice in a way that was firm yet filled with grace. Observing my mom meet the challenges of realizing she was stuck in this Static Phase planted a seed of confidence in my heart to look within myself, and maybe, just maybe, take a step forward too.

I (Debbie) was in the Static Phase most of my life until I started counseling and came to know Jesus Christ in my early 40s. I began my journey by looking into the mirror one day and saying to myself, "This is my third marriage. What is the common denominator in this equation?" I'd spent my whole life up to that point, and beyond, operating out of hurt and abandonment, trying to shield myself from sadness and pain. I made a promise to myself early in life believing it was far better to build a concrete wall around my heart and not get hurt than it was to be true to myself regarding emotions, vulnerability and authenticity.

That lie catapulted me straight into helping others to a fault so I would not have time or energy to look at myself. I believed it would be far too painful and selfish to do so. It was much easier to blame someone else and look at the speck in *their* eye while refusing to acknowledge the huge log in my own. Over time, that faulty belief left me in a place of emotional silence unable to recognize and utilize the beautifully designed voice that only God can give regarding our unique gifts and talents. I attempted to please others at the expense of what I truly desired – to be loved and accepted.

Unfortunately, the one thing I thought was keeping me safe and secure was the same thing stealing the joy, freedom, and peace that God designed for me to live in. What had once worked for me, and had allowed me to survive emotionally for so long, was no longer working. It was keeping me stuck in the unhealthy places I had always known.

In some ways, our unhealthy perceptions can feel safer because it is what we've known for so long. Sadly, the pain has to increase beyond an uncomfortable level before most of us are willing (and able) to move past the Static Phase to begin to learn, grow, stretch, and ultimately change.

The next five days of exploration will set the stage for you to begin the real process of honest self-assessment and personal contemplation, juxtaposed with what God says about you. If you find that you relate to most of the Static Phase concepts, our heart is to encourage you forward in your journey. Don't be afraid, the best is yet to come!

If, however, you recognize that these concepts have already been processed in your present personal life, we encourage you to listen for anything the Lord is further revealing to you. When we posture our heart toward empathy and compassion, we open up the opportunity to learn how we might be a helpful companion to another woman who may need a friend or mentor as she grows through her seasons of identity.

Self-Care Challenge

Continue to set aside time for self-care during your busy week. How is it impacting you? What do you observe differently about yourself as you set this important time aside? Have you thought about adding a few minutes in the morning and before you go to bed to deep breath and take a scan of your body? Try lying down flat on the ground with arms and legs fully relaxed. Notice if there is tension in your hands, shoulders, jaw, or face. Take a few deep breaths. Inhale for four counts, hold for four counts, and exhale for four counts. Open your heart to the Lord's leading. What are you feeling?

Leadership Connection

Take time this week to contemplate areas in your life that you may have moved through too quickly toward Advocacy and leading, but feel the fragility of a faulty foundation. Get real and honest about it. It could represent a wound that hasn't healed. You are worth taking time to repair. Remember you can't do this alone. Bring someone along in your development. The people you lead will benefit from your growth process.

Static

The Static Phase[6] of feminine development is perpetuated by both a deficiency of identity and strength, and minimal boundary formation. It feels right to accept things the way they are in terms of limited self-care, self-compassion and possible discrimination. A woman in this phase of feminine development will often fear what others might think of her and will look to others for identity definition and values structure. This phase can also be perpetuated by self-doubt and shame that is often disguised by tendencies to become enmeshed in subsequent relationships.

Due to the fact that female socialization (the interpersonal information she may have received growing up) can often include messages that perpetuate the idea that she cannot trust her own perceptions; a woman can, at times, feel powerless over her circumstances. She might see logically what is going on, but may not have the confidence to believe in herself or have access to the strength within to advocate for herself. A woman in the Static Phase can often have a disharmonious and fearful perception of men based upon prior experiences. Sometimes the underlying, subconscious issues of denial and resentment over not being heard or advocated for, can give way to subversive anger toward themselves and others. This can cause a woman to withdraw from authentic connection, yet feel conflicted about it. A woman in the Static Phase has a hard time believing her unique story matters.

Concerning spirituality, a woman in this phase tends to speak of her relationship with Christ in positive terms and is serving the Lord altruistically, yet she doesn't always know how to connect her service as being an outpouring of her truest self in Him. This can impact her ability to verbalize and truly believe in who she is in Christ. A woman in the Static Phase might feel very conflicted in her walk with Christ because she knows something needs to be developed in her, but may not know how to pursue it.

---

6. Research adapted to reflect a Christ-centered focus from Downing, N. E. and Roush, K. L., "From Passive Acceptance to Active Commitment: A Model of Feminist Identity Development for Women," *The Counseling Psychologist*, Vol. 13, No. 4, October 1985.

When a woman has traversed the Static Phase and begins to take some risks in terms of self-compassion, community, and self-care, she becomes receptive to the possibility of new perspectives.

Thoughts & Notes:

_____

_____

_____

_____

_____

_____

_____

_____

_____

_____

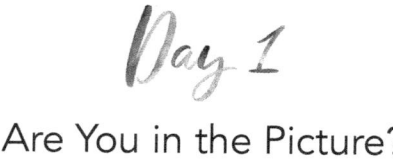

Day 1

Are You in the Picture?

Read Ephesians 3:14-21

When I think of all this, I fall to my knees and pray to the Father, the Creator of everything in heaven and on earth. I pray that from his glorious, unlimited resources he will empower you with inner strength through his Spirit. Then Christ will make his home in your hearts as you trust in him. Your roots will grow down into God's love and keep you strong. And may you have the power to understand, as all God's people should, how wide, how long, how high, and how deep his love is. May you experience the love of Christ, though it is too great to understand fully. Then you will be made complete with all the fullness of life and power that comes from God.

Now all glory to God, who is able, through his mighty power at work within us, to accomplish infinitely more than we might ask or think. Glory to him in the church and in Christ Jesus through all generations forever and ever! Amen. (NLT)

1. What phrase or message impacts you most in these verses?

_____

_____

2. Why do you think Paul would take the time to pray that we would have the power to understand the depth of God's love for us?

_____

_____

Seasons | Craft · Chaney · Rasa

3. Do you think, based on the words he chose, that Paul knew we might have a difficult time realizing our worth to God? Explain your thoughts.

_____

_____

One sunny California morning, I (Teri) sat and listened to a wonderful wife and mother, whom I'd been working with for a few weeks, tell me her story of the pain and frustration she was experiencing from her family interactions. After some time has passed, I asked, "If you stood back for a moment and took a snapshot of your family in these interactions, where are you in the picture?" This normally perky and responsive woman sat silent, and eventually began to cry. Between tears, she uttered softly, "To be honest, I'm either taking the picture and trying to make it all look good, or I'm not in the scene at all because I'm running around in the background attempting to keep everyone happy." It was a life-changing, lightbulb turned on, billboard-sized revelation of her current reality. For the first time, this beautiful woman was able to see where she allowed herself to be in her own environment and began to contemplate if that was where God intended her to be. She commented over and over how she couldn't believe the impact of that one mental picture and how it opened her heart to see something new.

4. Take some time to ponder the visual above. Where do you see yourself in the picture of *your* life? Is it where you want to be?

_____

_____

5. Do you believe it's where God wants you to be when you consider the words of Ephesians 3:14-21? What feelings are being stirred inside of you?

_____

_____

It is possible that a very complex story brought you to this moment in time. **The most important aspect of being able to look at our realities and not become overwhelmed by them is knowing that God's love for us is deep, wide, long and high.** It's also important to recognize if shame has crept in. (Remembering how our story may have included some perceptions or lies that came through wounds, traumas, or trials can help with this process.) Then we begin to let the love of Jesus open our hearts to allow His grace to envelop us. Give yourself some grace. This process of self-compassion takes time to develop.

6. What does it feel like to have compassion for yourself as you look at the picture of your life or current reality? *(If this is a new concept, we encourage you to reach out to a friend and ask them to walk with you as you commit to having a more compassionate view of your own personal life and development.)*

_____

_____

7. Think of some creative ways you can give yourself permission to demonstrate self-compassion this week that honors God as you honor His beautiful creation in you.

_____

_____

8. We encourage you to be intentional, to mentally "put yourself in the picture" of your current life journey and all the situations that come from that place. It can be helpful to begin to observe life in this way, to see how you feel about where you naturally gravitate in your daily environments in relation to others around you. Make some notes regarding how you feel about what you are noticing.

_____

_____

Be Loved

"See how very much our Father loves us, for he calls us his children, and that is what we are!" 1 John 3:1 (NLT)

Last week we took some time to think about the words in the passage above. Today, we are going to revisit this passage and continue to journey through the Static Phase of our growth model.

1. Having processed the foundational truth of your identity in Christ, and the power that lies and wounds can have to distort that truth, are you seeing this passage in a different way? What are you noticing in this moment when you read it out loud and "put yourself in the picture?" Explain.

_____

_____

Have you ever noticed that the meaning of words can change just by reading them a certain way, or by modifying the emphasis on certain syllables or groups of letters?

For example: We are nurtured many times in the word of God when we are called God's *beloved*, which essentially is a term of endearment, esteeming us, and helping us recognize we are worthy of His unconditional love. What is our part? Simply put, to *be* loved.

You might be thinking, *What does being loved have to do with the Static Phase?* What we discovered when talking with many girls and women was that they struggled with the concept of being worthy of the kind of love God offers. Few had difficulty believing God loved them, but to accept they were His *beloved* and fundamentally worthy of that kind of attention was often a different story.

We chose the symbol of intertwined circles to illustrate the concept of the Static Phase because when we, as women, have difficulty living our lives from the foundation of the love and acceptance of our truest selves in Christ, we get stuck and remain in a static state.

2. What feels "stuck" in your life right now? Is this a new challenge, or has it been there for a period of time?

_____

_____

3. What would change in your life if you began to fully live in this love and acceptance?

_____

_____

4. What are the barriers to you receiving God's unconditional love?

_____

_____

If you're anything like me (Debbie), not being able to *be* loved the way I was meant to be loved created self-doubt and shame. It was hard to have confidence in myself so, I relied on others for approval and direction. I had even experienced some messages growing up in school and in social situations that made me second-guess my ability to express my opinion based on my being female. (This was a common issue we heard when many women spoke about their lives.) This lack of confidence established during my childhood, coupled with my inability to see myself as worthy of love and acceptance, made it difficult to recognize that I was in a Static state in my personal and leadership growth, let alone know what to do about it. In other words, there was a part of me I hid away. I learned to manage my life around this persona so the outside looked as good as possible. The problem, though, is that I wasn't maturing in the deepest parts of my soul that had been wounded or broken. I molded myself into what I thought I needed to be, both to please others and to fit in. I felt like I had to continually look polished, put together, and smart. I was always performing to prove something to someone.

5. If you can relate to any part of the paragraph above, write your thoughts below.

_____

_____

_____

Consider these words from Dr. John Townsend in his book *Hiding from Love*:[7]

> Hiding always has some fruit, or symptom. In other words, you and I can detect hiding in our lives by the problems it causes. When we hide, a part of our character is pushed away from relationship into a spiritual darkness called isolation. The isolation of some part of our soul from love will always produce a problem.

6. Considering the statement above, have you ever, or are you now, experiencing the fruit (consequences) of hiding or isolating from love?

_____

_____

_____

_____

7. Dr. John Townsend, *Hiding From Love: How to Change the Withdrawal Patterns that Isolate and Imprison You*, Zondervan (1996).

7. Can you identify these problems? Write them below.

_____

_____

_____

_____

_____

8. Take some time to quietly contemplate the idea that you are beloved of God, and how much He wants you to receive that transformational love, not only on the outside of your life, but deep inside. If you are comfortable, share your thoughts with someone you trust.

_____

_____

_____

_____

_____

Day 3

What's OK, and What's NOT OK

Above all else, guard your heart, for everything you do flows from it. Keep your mouth free of perversity; keep corrupt talk far from your lips. Let your eyes look straight ahead; fix your gaze directly before you. Give careful thought to the paths for your feet and be steadfast in all your ways. Do not turn to the right or the left; keep your foot from evil.

Proverbs 4:23-27 (NIV)

The following is an excerpt from my journal when I (Rachel) was in college a few years ago:

I have been watching and observing how some of the girls at my university interact with others now that I have started working on the concept of Seasons with my mom. What I have noticed is that a lot of them, like me, are trying to find deeper facets of their personal identity. Many are relentlessly searching for something to make them feel secure in themselves and attaching themselves to whatever or whomever shows them any attention...whether it is good or not. When I've asked some of the girls about it, they speak of feeling alone. I've observed that many have little boundaries and get hurt easily, yet continue to put themselves in positions just to feel connected and secure. When I encourage them to have better personal boundaries, they think it's a good idea, yet they can't seem to follow through. I've observed that many young adults my age do not have an understanding of boundaries and they often put themselves in situations without even thinking about it, and then wonder why they keep getting hurt.

I, too, am on a journey of discovery of my truest identity. I am in continuous conversation with my boyfriend, my counselor, and others that I am accountable to, yet I also feel alone sometimes. I'm trying to learn to be ok with it so I can live a healthy, balanced life. I confess, it's very hard at times. I only know of the concept of boundaries because my parents have taken the time to walk me through it and help me process when I fail. I'm often criticized by some of the other people around me for not partying, or going out with lots of guys. I am observing that the more I have healthy boundaries in relationships, the more and more I am less like the majority of the people around me. I often wonder how girls my age understand true femininity and strength, and how they are possibly getting stuck without knowing or understanding why. If that's the case, and no one helps them through it, how will they impact the world around them?

1. After reading Proverbs 4:23-27 and my journal entry, what comes to mind? Circle or note below any key words or phrases from the verse that resonate with you.

_____

2. Who or what taught you what was OK and what was NOT OK in your life?

_____

_____

3. Take some time and list what you feel is OK and NOT OK in the context of your relationships and personal health below.

OK:

_____

_____

NOT OK:

_____

_____

In the book, *Boundaries*,[8] by Drs. Henry Cloud and John Townsend, the authors state that, "A boundary shows me where I end and someone else begins, leading me to a sense of ownership."

What I've come to understand more deeply through my life experiences, and by watching my parents navigate how to steward their lives, is that boundaries are essential. I also have come to understand that they are something we learn, either from someone who takes the time to explain or model them, or through life circumstances. I have experienced both. One is harder than the other.

4. How have you experienced the concept of boundaries in your life? Explain.

_____

_____

5. Explain in your own words how you are connecting the concepts of stewardship (ownership, responsibility) and boundaries.

_____

_____

6. How do you think being in a Static place in your life would either help or hinder this understanding?

_____

_____

_____

8. Dr. Henry Cloud and Dr. John Townsend, *Boundaries: When to Say Yes, How to Say No to Take Control of Your Life -Updated and Expanded*, Zondervan (2017).

You'll notice in the Static Phase description that it can feel right to accept things the way they have always been, even if we, as women, have suffered wounds in our identity, strength, and boundary structure. Some of the ways we are encouraging you to reframe your understanding is by putting yourself in the picture, having self-compassion, considering the impact of your life story, and accepting the deep and unconditional love of Christ.

7. What does the paragraph above mean to you? How are you processing this concept?

_____

_____

_____

_____

_____

8. Spend some time talking to a trusted friend about your personal reaction to your answer. How does it make you feel?

_____

_____

_____

_____

_____

Advance to Go

I (Teri) am sure that at some point in your life you have played the game, *Monopoly*. For our family, playing this classic game is a realistic glimpse into each of our unique personalities and competitive underpinnings. The truth is, you never know what is going to happen during one of our epic *Monopoly* game nights. One of the cards I love to receive during the game is the Chance card that reads, "Advance to Go." Doesn't everyone? This means that I get to skip past all the potential hazards and collect $200.

You might be wondering why I'm contemplating *Monopoly* in this daily prompt, but it connects perfectly to my past journey of limping through my personal development. You see, because I was unaware that I was in a static place deep inside my soul, I learned to manage my outward appearance in ways that maintained the status quo. I used a great deal of energy to keep things safe, and denied myself the beauty of appreciating my story and how the bad parts, as well as the good ones, were potential catalysts for growth. There was so much shame and doubt wrapped around my identity that being honest about how I was feeling was a non-option. I chose, instead, to take my Chance card and skip straight to the Advocacy Phase.

Later, we will learn more about what it means to develop through the growth phases to Advocacy. For now, it is easiest to view the Advocacy Phase as the culmination and consolidation of our maturing process. This is where we live, lead, and serve in true identity, strength, and authenticity. My problem was that, though I wanted to lead and serve others in this capacity, I didn't have the maturity (even as an adult) to support my vision and efforts. I was hemorrhaging from the inside out.

Let's consider Jesus' words to us in Mark 12: 28-31 (NLT):

> *"One of the teachers of religious law was standing there listening to the debate. He realized that Jesus had answered well, so he asked, 'Of all the commandments, which is the most important?'*
>
> *Jesus replied, 'The most important commandment is this: "Listen, O Israel! ,The Lord our God is the one and only Lord.And you must love the Lord your God with all your heart, all your soul, all your mind, and all your strength." The second is equally important: "Love your neighbor as yourself." No other commandment is greater than these.' "*

1. What does it mean to you to "love your neighbor as yourself?"

_____

_____

2. How do you feel about the following statement? "One way that we love ourselves is by taking time to allow Jesus to walk us through a discipleship journey of identity and maturity."

_____

_____

3. Where do you see yourself in the above statement?

_____

_____

Please hear my heart, I am in NO WAY saying that we shouldn't love and serve others. It is clear that it is the Lord's command. What I am trying to illuminate is the deeper "why" and "how" we are doing it. Simply put, the Lord loves us too much to allow us to stay static as His daughters. But the way that we grow and transform most often requires us to surrender in honesty and vulnerability to the challenging potential of discipleship. This can often feel hard or scary when we have suffered in our story.

Coming to terms with where we actually are in our present reality (or where someone we are helping through this process is) is the first step to growing through it into something new.

We need each other for this. We can't do it alone. I wonder if the verse above is alluding to the posture not only of loving and serving others in a ministry capacity, but also of the organic beauty of traveling together as His children in honest transformation and growth.

4. What stands out to you most in the above paragraph?

_____

_____

5. How are you seeing the words of Mark 12:28-31 in a deeper way? How does this impact you and the way you love and serve others?

_____

_____

_____

6. Where do you need help in your present growth journey?

_____

_____

_____

7. What might you need to focus on before you "Advance to Go?"

_____

_____

_____

Day 5

The Potential That Curiosity Brings

What we found when we talked with women of all ages about their personal journey of growth and identity, was that curiosity was present in the mindset of those who had an easier time "phasing" through the growth model scenarios in different seasons and situations throughout their life. This means that being open to the possibility of a new perspective and taking some steps to try new ways of approaching life was helpful for their feminine growth and discipleship in Christ.

In other words, being curious, or having a desire or open heart to discover and learn something new, is a healthy part of the transformational process.

I (Debbie) remember thinking it was best to have a strong opinion – right, wrong, or indifferent. *Just please have an opinion* was what I told myself based upon how I was socialized growing up. It wasn't until Teri Craft and Nancy Houston began to teach me how to be curious and try to hold both thoughts, and maybe the opposing opinion, that a whole new world of empathy and sincere compassion with regard to someone else's thought processes and feelings opened up, enabling me to see another's perspective. It felt so freeing, and much more authentic to be caring and loving toward someone, even if I disagreed. As I continue to learn about this process, I can begin to shift from subject to object. Meaning, it takes the focus off of what the person is saying and makes it more about the situation, or relationship, it represents. This ultimately enables me to be more empathetic and less offended.

The fascinating part is that I am just now beginning to see what a huge benefit and difference it makes in having deep, meaningful conversations. All without compromising our values and spiritual beliefs, simultaneously broadening our scope of knowledge, growth, and learning. It not only stretches us; it enhances our depth of relationship as women in all areas of leadership positions today, both in our workplace and in our homes. Learning to trust the process knowing that the pursuit of God is our ultimate goal, whatever paths our lives ultimately take. *"And we know that in all things God works for the good of those who love him, who have been called according to his purpose."* Romans 8:28 (NIV).

Let's consider the story of Mary's heart and curiosity in Luke 1: 26-56.

1. Focus on verse 34. What are you hearing through Mary's question?

_____

_____

2. Read verses 35-38. Describe this exchange in your own words.

_____

_____

3. What part did curiosity play in Mary's story?

_____

_____

4. What is her ultimate response in verses 46-56, even amidst the uncertainty of her present reality?

_____

_____

The truth is, curiosity was a catalyst in driving out fear and ushering in Mary's faith response to what would seem an impossible scenario presented to her by the angel, Gabriel. It unleashed the potential for an eye-opening experience, an "aha" moment, and a miracle of monumental proportion. Let's make it personal.

5. What in your life seems impossible?

_____

_____

6. What are the barriers in your perspective that stop you from being curious?

_____

_____

7. Commit to changing your posture to curiosity in one area of your life that is difficult right now. (Intentionally choosing to be curious about the outcome of a situation, curious about why you're seeing something the way you do, curious about how you are viewing or acting toward others, or curious about what God may be showing or teaching you through a circumstance... etc.)

_____

_____

8. Who will hold you accountable?

_____

_____

Week 4

Transition Introduction

The second component of the *Seasons* Four-Phase model is Transition. Transition is the place where our humanity intersects with God's sovereignty and, if we are open to it, we are forever changed. In other words, Transition is the rubber-hits-the-road, I'm in over my head, I can't believe this is happening, how did I get here, things will never be the same, kind of season. The truth is, we all have seasons of transition, and we have most likely observed or walked alongside other women who have been thrust into this environment as well.

> **What we would like to propose is the idea that transition is one of the best places to catapult transformational growth in our feminine identity formation.**

The problem is, it can be a very messy, sad, and ugly season for everyone involved. Therefore, a lot of us either try to outrun it, deny it, act out within it, or crumble under the weight of it. That is one of the reasons we chose a triangle as the graphic. It is not like Static, where there is repetitive movement and it can feel as if things are stagnant, or hovering. On the contrary, Transition has direction potential, and is often brought on by unforeseen events, a culmination of choices, or an illumination of truths. It's pointed and acute. Transition has a way of making things that were hidden come to light.

It's how we respond to transition that is everything...

In my (Teri's) past, I had little desire to ever experience anything that looked like friction, risk, or conflict. My internal make-up was geared toward fear and transactional acceptance, so you can imagine how hard I worked each day to keep the plates spinning to protect myself and everyone around me from any and all pain and suffering. (If you haven't guessed, I'm an Enneagram 7.) The problem was, I couldn't mature past a certain point because I essentially denied myself, and others I loved the most, the opportunity to learn. Think about the seasons in your life through which you grew or learned the most. What was meaningful about those seasons? If you're like most people, they likely included some measure of pain or difficulty. That's the unique fuel of Transition. The potential found when life presses in hard and something new in you has the opportunity to emerge.

For me (Rachel), a good portion of my teenage years were transitional. When I would even hear the word transition, it triggered a traumatic response within me. All the positive potential held within its definition was overshadowed by fear, anger, and confusion.

Transition was a sad reality that I felt every day as my family moved from one location to another, I suffered a myriad of personal and family losses, and I prayed the real prayer that my parents would make it through their journey of marriage recovery taking place right before my eyes. Transition caused all my insecurities to surface as I was faced with the reality that I was not in control. I tend to look for potholes on every road I travel. (Yes, I'm an Enneagram 6.) When I finally leaned into the process of change in my life with some safe people, I found strength I never knew existed inside of me.

For me (Debbie), transition was hard, just like lasting change can be hard for many of us. I felt as if it had to be black or white, one extreme or the other, for it to be a significant transition. Then I learned through a series of process groups and one-on-one intensives how it was possible to hold both. What I mean by that is staying in my own hula-hoop (as Nancy Houston says) while at the same time entering the transition of seeing things from a different perspective or lens. I didn't really know I had a boundary blind-spot until some very safe, wisdom-filled women were able to speak into my life.

One example involves my first marriage when I was faced with the devastating choice of having to move my physical location and uproot my entire life as I knew it, but not because of anything I had done. Because of my first husband's involvement in a corrupt business that led to his incarceration one short year after we were married. That situation forced me to look at the only life I had known and essentially start over at twenty-three, without the conscious awareness of the loss and grief that would follow. I believe this is where my anger started to boil deep beneath the surface while, simultaneously, new growth began without my awareness...until many years later. Hence, my boundary structure and transitional stage of needed growth into healthy relationships was birthed unbeknownst to me.

Can we be honest? Transition is hard. It's the venue of growth that most of us would rather omit from our lives. But as we mentioned previously, it holds within its unique moment in time an intersection, a possibility, a choice. We found that many of the girls and women we journeyed with who traversed this phase successfully spoke of their seasons of transition as being excruciating, yet productive. The difficulty they faced, even if it was tragic, birthed something they never thought possible. This reminds us of our Contemplation of Mary's experience and her curiosity in Luke 1 from Week 3, Day 5. What's important to note, however, is the fact that the women we talked to and journeyed with, and we can agree from our own life experiences as well, didn't navigate their seasons of transition perfectly. There was a fair bit of crying, cussing, doubting, lashing out, and even isolating at times. From the fire of adversity was rising an authenticity that just wasn't refined yet. What is the difference between these women and those who stuff emotions or compartmentalize through Transition and ultimately end up back in a Static state?

Two important words. **VULNERABILITY** and **CONNECTION**.

Here's where it gets important for each of us to take note. If we all have seasons of transition, and we know that they are hard and can produce some sharp edges on our exteriors, then we, as women, are called upon to open our hearts to one another. To create safe environments for honesty, vulnerability, and connection so we and other women and girls can navigate growth in a way that is healthy and authentic.

Self-Care Challenge

You've been diving deep into some difficult memories and emotions. Are you staying committed to taking care of your mind, body, and spirit? How are the deep breathing and intentional self-care strategies working for you? What do you need to add or subtract from your routine?

Leadership Connection

As a frontrunner, it can be easy to use our gifts and competencies to plow ahead. Remember, leaders can feel stuck in an area of life as well. This week, take some time to assess areas that, for one reason or another, you feel unable to move forward in. Are you, for example, struggling in an area that may require you to grieve the loss of something? Is there resistance based upon a faulty belief system that needs to be addressed? Do you need rest or help?

Transition

The Transition Phase[9] is often initiated and accelerated by a crisis, difficulty, or acknowledgement of past wounding or trauma. This dislodges a woman from the Static Phase into the knowledge that she is unable to live in denial any longer with the conflicts within her, and in the world around her. When a woman has been receptive during the previous phase, traversing Transition is easier on all levels. Because the Transition Phase is essentially an eye-opening experience, it can be catalytic when approached with a level of curiosity and optimism. It is in this phase that anger often rises to the surface and can become a primary feeling, with regret often becoming a secondary motivator. This can lead to two dysfunctional patterns. The first sees the woman pulling back from authentic connection, and the second is the possibility of creating a false persona of strength that is actually based upon subversive or expressed anger. This can sometimes be displayed as a misuse or abuse of power to others she comes in contact with, or is in relationship with.

Positive growth in this phase requires the risk of vulnerability, an openness to explore what healthy separateness and personal identity mean, and the willingness to address boundary formation in relationships. Women in the Transition Phase often have skeptical and overgeneralized views of men if they are not actively growing in their personal identity and discipleship. The Transition Phase is typified by a life crisis juxtaposed with a woman's ability to get curious about her life and reach out in vulnerable relationship, especially with other women who have gone before her. When she thinks of her story, it can be scary and overwhelming, or even feel shameful to her. This new exploration and curiosity open a pathway for the possibility of healthy grieving to take place, making way for greater identity, strength, and optimism.

Concerning spirituality, a woman in this phase will have the opportunity to open her heart to grieve and grow through a newfound vulnerability brought on by suffering or, conversely, get stuck in transactional relational patterns that look like strength and vision, but which are undergirded

---

9, Research adapted to reflect a Christ-centered focus from Downing, N. E. and Roush, K. L., "From Passive Acceptance to Active Commitment: A Model of Feminist Identity Development for Women," *The Counseling Psychologist*, Vol. 13, No. 4, October 1985.

by anger and doubt. Grace is a concept spoken of, yet little is reserved for herself in this phase. This has the potential to make her discipleship journey feel hopeless and confusing. The key is creating safe environments for exploration of what it means to "be" rather than "do." The mentor or "sage" relationship, as well as process group participation, is of utmost importance for a woman traveling through the Transition Phase.

Thoughts & Notes:

_____

_____

_____

_____

_____

_____

_____

_____

_____

Day 1

Winter

"It is a season when death's victory can seem supreme:
few creatures stir, plants do not visibly grow and nature feels like our enemy.
And yet the rigors of winter, like the diminishments of autumn,
are accompanied by amazing gifts."[10]

I (Rachel) can't tell you exactly when the dark foreboding clouds appeared on the horizon of my life. All I can say is that I knew things had changed, and I was terrified. I spent days wondering if the darkness was ever going to leave or if I had the strength to make it through. It all came to a head in the middle of January when I had a full load of classes at the university.

I had just recuperated from an injury, and the indoor college track and field competitions were ramping up. My mental health was declining, though I didn't want to admit it at the time. I thought I had nowhere to turn and honestly believed I had no choice but to deal with the oncoming clouds on my own. The façade I exhibited on the outside, however, was so convincing that people just kept telling me to "push through it". Deep inside, I knew it was not going to go away that easy.

Can I be vulnerable with you? There is a real stigma around mental health issues in our world. Doctors, surgeons, and physical therapists were anxious to help when I hurt my ankle as a Division I athlete; but when I was falling apart emotionally, not sleeping, losing weight, and feeling utterly depressed, I was pretty much on my own.

Have you or someone you know ever been there? It's like living in a perpetual state of Winter with no hope of Spring. When I finally broke down and let someone really know what I was going through, and I stopped running from my fears, the pathway forward started to become clear. With the help of some safe people, I grabbed ahold of my future by coming to terms with the reality of my present mess. Through the barren and leafless trees, I caught a glimpse of something on the horizon I had not seen before... freedom.

The vulnerable journey I embarked upon in those winter months allowed me to process some

---

10. Parker J. Palmer, Let Your Life Speak: Listening for the Voice of Vocation, Jossey-Bass (1999) 101.

deep pain from my past and come to terms with the way I was coping in the present. I slowly moved from a season of depression and sadness into a place of appreciation and contentment.

There were some difficult days, but being able to move through the Winter season, instead of just running around it, or from it, allowed me to experience the true gift of growth in a way that is difficult to describe in words. It is now my deepest joy and honor to walk with others through their Winter seasons as a helping professional. I know what it is like to see the clouds roll in. But, guess what? You are not alone, and you don't need to stay in the shadow.

Consider Ecclesiastes 3:1,4:

> "For everything there is a season, a time for every activity under heaven...
> A time to cry and a time to laugh. A time to grieve and a time to dance." (NLT)

1. In light of what we're learning, what does this passage mean to you personally?

_____

_____

_____

2. Have you given yourself permission to grieve? Why or why not?

_____

_____

_____

Think about this statement about Transition from the Week 4 Introduction:

"The problem is, it can be a very messy, sad, and ugly season for everyone involved. Therefore, a lot of us either try to outrun it, deny it, act out within it, or crumble under the weight of it. That is one of the reasons we chose a triangle as the graphic. It is not like Static, where there is repetitive movement and it can feel as if things are stagnant, or hovering. On the contrary, Transition has direction potential, and is often brought on by unforeseen events, a culmination of choices, or an illumination of truths. It's pointed and acute. Transition has a way of making things that were hidden come to light.

It's how we respond to transition that is everything...

3. Take a few minutes to quiet your heart and breathe deeply. Then share below how you are now responding, or have in the past responded, to seasons of transition.

_____

_____

_____

4. How does the idea of Transition having "directional potential" make you feel?

_____

_____

5. Have you or someone you know ever been treated poorly while navigating the difficult season of transition? Explain.

_____

_____

_____

A Time to Grieve

We can rejoice, too, when we run into problems and trials,
for we know that they help us develop endurance.
And endurance develops strength of character,
and character strengthens our confident hope of salvation.
And this hope will not lead to disappointment.
For we know how dearly God loves us,
because he has given us the Holy Spirit to fill our hearts with his love.

Romans 5:3-5 (NLT)

We may know the truth found in Romans 5:3-5 – that our trials will ultimately lead to hope. But just *knowing* something doesn't change us from the inside out.

It's the process of persevering and surrendering, acknowledging and relinquishing in our trials, that ushers in transformation.

This most often takes us through the process of grieving.

I (Teri) have heard it said, "Make the effort to change what you can, and grieve what you cannot." Seasons of transition often put us in a position to test this statement. The sobering realization that we are face to face with the "uninvited guest" called death, loss, betrayal, abuse, oppression, illness, or change often forces us to make this very choice. Grief can even make its appearance in times of joy, when one dream awakens, but we must say goodbye to another. These are the moments that ultimately produce great potential for our identity growth as women. We are challenged to look at our foundational belief system to discover who we really are and where our hope is ultimately grounded.

Here's the truth.

Grieving is the part of the growth process that denotes movement. It has the power to take us from a static and stuck place, to freedom, acceptance, and empowerment in our own unique stories.

1. What stands out the most to you from Romans 5:3-5? Explain.

_____

_____

_____

2. What does it mean to you to "rejoice" when you encounter problems and trials? What circumstances have shaped that view?

_____

_____

_____

I sit with women experiencing loss and grief on a daily basis. Overwhelmingly, I hear them express shame and fear in relation to the process of grieving. Things really begin to shift for them in terms of healing and growth, however, when they allow themselves to take an inventory of their losses and get real with the pain. But that's not the end of the story. Jesus wants us to release those losses to Him and allow Him to hold the emotions, memories, and painful moments. Then, if we are open to it, He gracefully offers peace, hope, and a new perspective that includes the possibility of growth.

What can often hold us back from grieving is the thought that we must be perfect, or that we are letting others, and God, down. **The truth is, we must** feel...to heal. If you have ever struggled like me with the thought of grieving, it's time to examine Jesus' own model to us in Matthew 26:36-43.

3. What do you notice about Jesus' posture and emotional state in these verses? Underline or circle each phrase or sentence in which you detect an aspect of His grieving or His emotional connection to His reality.

_____

_____

4. Describe in your own words how you see Him navigating His grief.

_____

_____

5. What does this mean to you as a woman who is on the path of growth and maturity?

_____

_____

_____

Another great perspective is found in the book, *How People Grow,* by Dr. Henry Cloud and Dr. John Townsend. "Grief," they state, "is something we enter into. But its voluntary nature is not the only thing that sets grief apart from other kinds of suffering. The other difference is that grief is the one that heals all the others. It is the most important pain there is. This is why God calls us to enter into it voluntarily. It heals. It restores. It changes things that have gone bad."[11]

Drs. Cloud and Townsend expand on that statement by encouraging us to reach out to others for support as we grieve and create the time and space for this to happen in a healthy way.

_____

11. Dr. Henry Cloud and Dr. John Townsend, *How People Grow: What the Bible Reveals About Personal Growth,* Zondervan (2009) 228.

6. Take some time to begin the process of making a Grief Inventory. These are losses or painful memories you need to grieve in order to move forward in your journey of growth. This initial inventory, or list, will be the beginning of a healthy discipline that we encourage you to enter into for the rest of your life in different seasons, as losses inevitably come your way. Remember that you must give yourself time and space to do this, as well as bring others along in your process. We also recommend dealing with one loss at a time so you don't get overwhelmed. As with any process, if it gets too intense, we advise you to seek help from a counselor, if needed.

_____

_____

_____

_____

_____

_____

_____

_____

_____

What's Vulnerability Got To Do With It?

Yesterday we took the time to discuss what it means to grieve our losses as we navigate transitional seasons in our lives.

Simply put, grieving what we cannot change is a healthy part of our growth process as women.

Our stories are important, yet aspects of our life narratives can be scary, sad, or feel shameful when left without resolution. This can lead us to get stuck and potentially revert back to the familiar scenario and belief system found in the Static Phase.

The key to moving forward is vulnerability.

Seasons of transition have a way of getting our attention and often open us up for a deeper look at what we believe about ourselves, God, and others. It takes vulnerability to willingly unlock some of those beliefs and wounds. Remember the exercise we did in Week Two, when we wrote down our tragedies, traumas, and trials, and any lies that we believed because of them? Transition is where we look at the lies close-up and decide which direction we want to go.

1. Review the Week Two, Day Three *A Glance in the Rearview Mirror* exercise. Take some time to look at the tragedies, traumas, and trials you listed. Is there anything you still need to grieve?

_____

_____

_____

_____

2. Now look at the lies that came out of these trials. What would you like to see happen in your life today in relation to any of the lies you still believe about yourself and others? Explain.

_____

_____

_____

_____

I (Teri) understood this journey of vulnerability, the moment in time when I finally allowed God and some safe people in on my process of transition. I still vividly remember the eye-opening moment when I realized my life had forever changed. My marriage had been fractured by betrayal, our family was devastated, and our ministry was a dream washed away. I had been thrust into transition by a tornado of circumstance and I sat wondering, "How did I get here?" The next thought was, "Who am I in this mess, and do I have the strength to make it through?" That is where I began to get real with the "me" I didn't yet know… the Teri deep inside that Jesus was encouraging in the present, based on the future of what He knew to be true about me. I just couldn't see it in the wasteland that lay before me. But with time, some amazing people, and the Lord's great care, I began to release what had been bound, unearth what had been buried, and expose what had been established as lies in the framework of my soul, until I found peace and joy in who I was, no matter what trial I had to endure. Here are some thoughts from my journal at the time.

> This time of recovery and place of dependence will always be special to me, because, in spite of the chaos, I found a peace and presence that felt as close to heaven on earth as I have experienced. I laid my burdens down and found new life in the process. This new life is special and sacred. Regardless of what the future holds, I know I will carry this with me for the rest of my life.[12]

_____

12. James Craft and Teri Craft, *EXPOSED: A Journey of Renewal and Hope,* Pure Desire Ministries International, Gresham, Oregon (2020).

3. Are you now walking through, or have you ever experienced, the Transition Phase of development? If so, describe the circumstances below.

_____

_____

_____

4. How do you feel about this situation? Have you told anyone about it?

_____

_____

Do you know what is really vulnerable? Realizing and confessing that you might just be a bit angry about what has happened to you or to someone you love that got you to this point in your journey. We want you to know that "It's OK *not* to be OK." The goal, however, is not to stay there. To be fair, I don't think anyone wants to stay stuck in their pain or slide back into a Static state of personal development, but we all have potential defense mechanisms. These can look like denial, repression, compartmentalization, avoidance, isolation or passive aggression, and can move in subtly to divert our true feelings at any moment making it harder to grow through the transitional circumstances we are experiencing. Again, the prescription is vulnerability. The problem, though, is that anger, sadness, and frustration can be messy. So messy, in fact, that we would rather not show that side of us. Sometimes we are even encouraged to grin and bear it while, at the same time, the Lord is calling us to vulnerably face it with a safe community as our support system. Need an example of authenticity and real-life response... even when it is raw?

Let's consider Naomi. Read Ruth 1:19-21:

5. How would you describe Naomi's feelings? Have you ever felt that way before? If so, what were the circumstances?

_____

_____

6. As you continue to read the rest of the book of Ruth, you see that, though Naomi was emoting her grief, and maybe a little bit of anger, she was not forsaken by God. What does that mean for you?

_____

_____

Seasons of transition can often provoke intense feelings of anger. But anger is often the symptom of a deeper issue of fear, or it signals the need for us to grieve some painful memories or losses. *Facing it* is what moves us forward.

7. Can you make the connection between a vulnerable expression of anger and grieving in a healthy community of supportive people with progressing forward in the phases of feminine growth? Explain your thoughts.

_____

_____

_____

_____

Day 4

Yard Work

We previously explored the concept of boundaries in Week Three, Day Three. Today we are going to dive in a little deeper to discuss how boundary formation and identity growth are both important factors in traversing the Four-Phase *Seasons* model.

In our discussions with women of all ages, we found that transition, being the eye-opening season that it is, often brings clarity to many women regarding their boundary structure deficits.

This is due to numerous factors. But something that came up often, was the real-life pain many of the women felt as they pondered how they allowed certain things to happen in their lives, despite the fact they weren't completely comfortable with it. Or the reality that they were just too scared to do anything about their situations and tried really hard to fix everything. Then when trials surfaced, they got curious about what they believed, or they started to gain more self-awareness regarding their true feelings, and they were faced with a choice. Two questions often voiced by these women were, "Who am I in this?" and "Who do I want to be moving forward?"

I (Debbie) grew up as the middle child. I always wanted to help people, please others, and make everyone around me happy so I would be accepted. Fans of Enneagram would easily guess that I am a solid 2 on the personality chart. This can pose a real challenge with boundaries and co-dependency. I knew what I had done my whole life. I just didn't understand why until I was well into my mid- to later-50s. I had learned to perform to feel accepted, loved, and valued. My performance was tied to the love that my mom (especially) showed me. If I was a good little girl, people around me would be happy, and I would feel loved. So began the messages that I perceived and received, that, subsequently, birthed inside of me the reinforced behavior I would consistently display.

I did not believe I was loved unconditionally the way Jesus loves me because I was raised to believe that showing emotion was a negative thing that made me appear weak. I was taught to pull myself up by my bootstraps and get on with it, to be strong and not depend on anyone, especially a man. I was hushed and told many times to "dry it up or I would be given something to cry about." Many years later, I learned what healthy boundaries look like and began to incorporate them in my life. Utilizing healthy boundaries helped me to find my voice, a voice I didn't even know I had lost. I was finally able to stand and speak on behalf of what I truly believed, to share my personal value and deep convictions, hence, my truest self. What I didn't realize was just how powerful, healthy, and beautiful that could be.

The truth is boundaries and identity are symbiotic. They are related and support one another in keeping us healthy as we live authentic lives displaying our truest selves in Christ.

Here's what Dr. Cloud and Dr. Townsend say about boundaries from their best-selling book, *Boundaries*.

> Any confusion of responsibility and ownership in our lives is a problem of boundaries. Just as homeowners set physical property lines around their land, we need to set mental, physical, emotional, and spiritual boundaries for our lives to help us distinguish what is our responsibility and what isn't.[13]

1. How does this relate to you and your story?

_____

_____

2. How does the imagery of our being "homeowners" and setting up "property lines around our land," help you to understand boundaries?

_____

_____

This idea of responsibility and ownership is directly related to our identity in Christ.

---

13. Dr. Henry Cloud and Dr. John Townsend, *Boundaries: When to Say Yes, How to Say No to Take Control of Your Life -Updated and Expanded*, Zondervan (2017) 27.

Read Romans 8:15-17a:

So you have not received a spirit that makes you fearful slaves. Instead, you received God's Spirit when he adopted you as his own children. Now we call him, 'Abba, Father.' For his Spirit joins with our spirit to affirm that we are God's children. And since we are his children, we are his heirs. In fact, together with Christ we are heirs of God's glory. (NLT)

3. Circle or underline all the words or phrases that connect us in relationship and identity to God.

_____

_____

4. If we are connected to God in relationship, identity, and image, how do boundaries fit into our stewardship of that sacred truth? Explain.

_____

_____

5. How could the lack of boundary structure impact your growth process?

_____

_____

The question we hear most from women regarding boundaries is, "Are boundaries okay for Christians?" The answer is, Yes! Setting limits is a healthy expression of our transformational walk with God.

When we can steward what He has created in us, we can truly impact the world around us.

6. Sit quietly for a few minutes. What words come to mind when you think of your life without boundaries?

_____

_____

7. Now imagine your life with good, healthy boundaries. What words come to mind?

_____

_____

Note: If you'd like to really understand this concept more fully, we recommend reading Boundaries *and completing the accompanying workbook. It takes some time to get these ideas working in our lives. Give yourself grace.*

Here's something to think about. Sometimes we can confuse anger with boundaries. We want to make sure that we are maturing properly and not just acting out in anger. An example of a healthy expression of anger is when we can *respond* to situations with others and not *react.* This includes:

- Being able to assess our root emotions. "What am I feeling right now?"
- Taking the time to consider everyone involved in the situation and make a healthy interpretation based upon reality and clarity. "Why am I feeling this way?"
- Making a choice that represents your best "you" in Christ.
- Responding appropriately, and if you don't, owning it.
- Taking time to cool down, pray, journal, or talk to someone.

Together

Have you ever noticed that when we, as women, find ourselves in seasons of transition, we often isolate? If that has ever happened to you, you're not alone. People, and the world around us, can seem very scary when we are in a fragile state of existence. All three of us know how this feels firsthand. From each of our unique vantage points, we longed to reach out and have someone embrace us in our time of need and, at the same time, expended a great deal of energy to guard ourselves to the point of isolation. We agreed that even standing in a crowded room felt excruciating, as if we carried a burden that no one else could understand.

Seasons of transition are essentially moments in time that hold within them great potential for change. In the same breath, these seasons can also be gut-wrenching, disheartening, and excruciating. There are, however, a few things that can make these moments come to life in terms of our transformational journey as women. We have worked through some of these concepts for the last few days. Today we touch upon the true power found in relationship and community.

Consider these words by Dr. Townsend from his book, *Hiding from Love:*

> The Bible proclaims our need for connection. At the deepest spiritual and emotional level, we are beings who need safety and a sense of belonging in our three primary relationships: God, self, and others.
>
> **Perhaps the number one root of emotional disorders is that some part of the self is isolated from relationship.** [14]

1. Do the words above relate to you today or in past times of transition? Explain.

_____

_____

14. Dr. John Townsend, *Hiding From Love: How to Change the Withdrawal Patterns that Isolate and Imprison You,* Zondervan (1996) 34-35.

2. What are/were the reasons you felt isolated?

_____

_____

_____

3. Take a moment to review Week Two, Day Three and the *Seasons of Trials* exercise. Are any of the reasons you are tempted to isolate from relationship connected to the lies that came out of your wounds or trials?

_____

_____

_____

4. What are you feeling with regard to the connection between relationship and growth?

_____

_____

_____

Read Ecclesiastes 4:9-12:

Two people are better off than one, for they can help each other succeed. If one person falls, the other can reach out and help. But someone who falls alone is in real trouble. Likewise, two people lying close together can keep each other warm. But how can one be warm alone? A person standing alone can be attacked and defeated, but two can stand back-to-back and conquer. Three are even better, for a triple-braided cord is not easily broken. (NLT)

5. Circle or underline all the words or phrases that have to do with the power of relationship in our lives.

_____

_____

6. What does this passage mean to you? How does it make you feel?

_____

_____

7. How does it relate to your personal story?

_____

_____

_____

Remember in Day Three of this week's prompt when we discussed the real possibility of anger rising to the surface in seasons of transition? Difficult times can make us feel out of control, damaged, or even victimized. This can surface in anger expressed outward, but it can also be shoved inward and repressed, causing numerous emotional and physical symptoms.

In order to move forward through the phases of feminine development, we must be able to get in touch with anger, sadness, and loss. The key, however, is not to do it alone. We need each other!

Personally, as I (Debbie) reflect on this, I am reminded of when I first started with a Leadership Processing Group about five years ago. What a wonderful opportunity and safe space to express what I didn't even realize I had to grieve or do an inventory for! Participating in that group allowed me to truly get angry and get in touch with the deeper parts of sadness and loss that I didn't even realize I had choked down or buried so deeply within. When I was young, any emotion I attempted to express was often squelched. I'm now 62 years old. Fortunately, relationships are handled much differently today than they were when I grew up. We did not have the benefit of curious or inquisitive parents who took time to try to understand why we felt the way we did. In the late-50s and early-60s, parents often did not have the luxury of time to focus on emotional, physical, or relational needs. Life was more about simply making ends meet. Children were expected to do what they were told and pull themselves up by their bootstraps. Much later in life I learned the beauty of transitioning into being more vulnerable and transparent, and ultimately investing in my own self-awareness, opening a pathway to understanding my *reactions* as opposed to *responses* to certain situations or triggers. As I continue to be curious and grow into a healthier woman today, I see growth and health in my emotional, physical, and spiritual wellness.

Without the expression of healthy community in our times of growth, we can get stuck or fall back into a Static state. This can look like our repressing our voice and taking all our energy to focus on other people's needs, neglecting our own. Sometimes this is done for altruistic ideals, but sometimes it is done to keep ourselves and our environments safe. An unhealthy option is to lash out to protect ourselves from further pain. Unfortunately, this just perpetuates hurt for everyone involved.

As noted in the introduction for this week's focus of the Transition Phase, making a choice to face our pain and reach out in vulnerability and community is essential to our growth and maturity through this process.

8. Who will help you walk through this season of Transition, or who are you walking alongside in theirs?

_____

_____

_____

_____

Our next growth phase is called Balance.

The bridge from Transition to Balance hinges on honesty, vulnerability, and community.

Each of these concepts is deep and wide and is not mastered in a single sitting. These are life-long pursuits. Our prayer is that you will take the opportunity to start to contemplate how these concepts are currently a part of your life expression, and how you can continue to grow in them. One way that has been helpful for us in our journey of healing and growth has been to be a part of a process group or small group. This gave us the chance to be honest in a safe environment, to own our story, and have people to walk with us as we moved forward. If you don't currently have one in your community, we encourage you to start one and use this study to begin the discussion.

Week 5

Balance Introduction

Balance. Just saying the word feels right as it rolls off the tongue. Consider your best life where all of the daily details are in alignment, equally distributed, and there's fertile ground for growth. You're at peace with whatever comes your way. Isn't it a wonderful thought? *This* is the essence of Balance and, as our third phase of development, is the substantive arena where things begin to fall into place. After a season of Transition, brought on by trials or revelation, the fruit of our lives now has the opportunity to develop. It is out of that transitional journey of perseverance in our lives that Balance can reach its full potential.

We chose the graphic of a plant to symbolize the season of Balance. Though we may take for granted the crucial variables that align to create an environment where a seed grows into a healthy plant that bears life-giving fruit, the process is no less complex. Have you thought much about that lately? The painstaking process that goes into the rich bounty of what we consume on a daily basis? The concept is similar to our own lives when we consider the process of discovery and development that leads to an environment of growth that sprouts from the inside out. The journey we navigate through the wind, rain, and scorching sun of circumstances ultimately yields freedom, abundant life, and strength. How do we know when this has occurred? One simple word...Balance.

As three unique women, we have experienced this excruciating, yet beautifully organic, unfolding in our own lives. What we've come to cherish is the peace and potential that ascended from the ashes meant to derail and destroy our unique identities in Christ.

You see, Balance has everything to do with holding both the good and the difficult seasons that come our way, and allowing wholeness to emerge.

Consider this passage:

May God himself, the God who makes everything holy and whole, make you holy and whole, put together – spirit, soul, and body – and keep you fit for the coming of our Master, Jesus Christ. The One who called you is completely dependable. If he said it, he'll do it! 1 Thessalonians 5:23-24 (MSG)

Our Creator, the One who knit us together in our mother's womb, has provided a way for us to grow and mature in and through all the seasons we experience. It is He who makes us whole. As a seed breaks forth from the soil in its perfect timing, so will we, as women of God. Not hindered by the fierce storms or circumstance that hit us head on or lulled into self-sufficiency by the warmth of success. Balance sees us moving forward in peace brought on by the trustworthy process of our Lord.

Self-Care

Are you setting aside time each day to rest, recuperate, and listen to what your heart and body need? We encourage you to step back from the busyness of your life and assess what could possibly be neglected in practical areas of your self-care as well. Have you made your annual women's health appointments? How long has it been since you've seen the dentist, optometrist, or chiropractor, or even had your financial situation evaluated? These are all part of your overall self-care strategy.

Leadership

When was the last time you partnered with other professionals to speak life or bring growth into your area of influence? Have you considered having an executive coach support your efforts to foster team bonding or organizational culture? Do the individuals you lead know that you care about their family, their marriages, and emotional health? If so, how would they benefit from hearing regularly from a licensed therapist? What would it be like to have a team that understood the importance of having personal financial goals, or healthy exercise and nutrition routines? The list is endless, and we encourage you to partner with others in your community to bring care and growth to your organization in ways you may not have considered before. This has the potential to bring balance in the workplace and beyond.

Balance

The Balance Phase[15] sees a woman growing in her ability to integrate the difficulties of life into an overall positive outlook. She is able to grieve losses as they come and take personal inventories when needed. She is also able to own her story with authenticity. A woman in the Balance Phase can identify oppression and relational tension, yet, still moves to respond appropriately without being overtaken by anger. She is open to the creation of a system of values that will serve as a foundation for moving forward into the next phase of development. As with all the phases, there is a risk of getting wounded in her areas of greatest giftedness, yet, she is willing to take a leap of faith.

A woman in Balance lives with intentional pause and leaves room for personal reflection, self-care, and relational connectedness.

As she phases through Balance, she is able to grow in her unique qualities and can verbalize and conceptualize aspects of her personal identity. Boundaries are seen as an integral part of her life, and she is able to work alongside men and not carry any stigma or stereotypes of them. Vulnerability and authenticity are something a woman in Balance is actively seeking as a means of personal expression and, when there are hindrances, she allows herself to be curious and not become judgmental with herself and others.

Concerning spirituality, a woman in the Balance Phase of feminine development is moving toward the ability to live in, and relate with, authentic love, gratitude, and vulnerability. She is beginning to really see Scripture through the lens of grace, first and foremost, for herself, and then outward as an expression of the overflow of Christ's grace she has received. She sees her story as wrapped around the gospel message and is beginning to see her identity in Christ as her utmost discipleship goal. Contemplation becomes a normal part of her spiritual journey with the Lord as she unveils shame's longstanding stronghold over her life. A woman in this phase will benefit from maintaining

---

15. Research adapted to reflect a Christ-centered focus from Downing, N. E. and Roush, K. L., "From Passive Acceptance to Active Commitment: A Model of Feminist Identity Development for Women," *The Counseling Psychologist,* Vol. 13, No. 4, October 1985.

connection with a mentor and/or process group, but also accepts the encouragement to begin to use her gifts in a way that impacts others from a place of authenticity.

Thoughts & Notes:

_____

_____

_____

_____

_____

_____

_____

_____

_____

_____

Living in Reality

I've heard it said that "reality is our best friend if we let it be." Let's face it, though, reality can be both excruciating and exhilarating. It can be hard to face when it bumps up against our fears or expectations. But if we pause for a moment, close our eyes, open our heart, and take a few deep breaths, we will connect with the truth that reality is where God does His most profound transformational work in our lives.

I can remember like it was yesterday, that spring day I found myself running as fast as I could down a quiet street in Hawaii Kai after receiving news from my husband that he had been unfaithful in our marriage. As hard as I tried to run away from the aftermath, I could not outrun the truth of what that reality meant to me personally, and for my marriage and family. From where, and how, did the healing for my broken story eventually come? It came through a journey of accepting the reality I was facing, and allowing God to heal and grow me at the point of impact. Right at the place I didn't want to acknowledge was real, but had to, in order to move forward. My husband did the same thing in his own life as well. Through this heartbreaking, beautiful, and challenging encounter with reality, we were both able to grow in places we never thought possible.

Navigating Balance in our lives as women means that we are intentionally empowering ourselves to deal with all the facets of our reality. Even if those realities are hard and we've spent a lifetime trying to outrun them.

Today we will take some time to understand the concept more fully, so that you can begin to make this kind of awareness and process part of your everyday life.

1. What realities are you facing today?

_____

_____

2. How do you feel about those realities?

_____

_____

3. Take a minute and allow yourself to extend kindness and curiosity toward yourself regarding how you feel. What does this grace do for you in relation to sitting with your realities?

_____

_____

4. Who can safely help you navigate these realities?

_____

_____

In his book, *The Emotionally Healthy Leader*, Pete Scazzero describes the truth that everyone has a shadow. "Your shadow is the accumulation of untamed emotions, less-than-pure motives and thoughts, that, while largely unconscious, strongly influence and shape your behaviors. It is the damaged but mostly hidden version of who you are."[16] Have you ever thought about the fact that it is in our "shadow" places that we often hide or ignore our realities, only to find that they grow uncontrollably and exponentially?

In the Balance Phase of growth, we as women come to terms with the "damaged and mostly hidden" places inside of us and begin to shine the light of God's grace, kindness, and mercy, so daily growth and transformation can occur in our lives.

Pete Scazzero notes that we often get good at protecting these broken places through *maneuvers*. He writes, "Maneuvers can be categorized into a few major categories—denial, minimizing, blaming yourself, blaming others, rationalizing, distracting, or projecting anger outward."[16] In the counseling world, we call them defense mechanisms, and they essentially render us ineffective against the transforming potential of reality when they are out of our awareness or just plain out of control.

In the space below take some time to contemplate how these specific "maneuvers," or defense mechanisms, are at work in your life. Take care. This exercise requires vulnerability, honesty, and a whole lot of kindness with yourself to explore.

Denial –
_____

Minimizing –
_____

Blaming Yourself –
_____

Blaming Others –
_____

Rationalizing –
_____

Distracting –
_____

Projecting Outward –
_____

5. What are you noticing as you explore this exercise? Are you leaving room for grace and curiosity instead of shame and condemnation?
_____

_____

_____

---

16. Scazzero, Peter, *The Emotionally Healthy Leader*, Zondervan (2015) 55, 61.

The beauty of this kind of journey is that you do not have to take it alone. Process what you are learning about yourself in context of navigating reality, and bring someone on the journey with you.

6. Contemplate this verse: "Knowing what is right is like deep water in the heart; a wise person draws from the well within." Proverbs 20:5 (MSG)

_____

_____

_____

_____

_____

_____

Reflect

As we walk through Balance and allow ourselves to process the good as well as the bad in our lives, doesn't it feel like we can finally take a deep breath and reflect? Morgan Harper Nichols said, "Notice the beauty of blooming flowers and the dried ones, too. Hold both grief and joy. Trust that grace will find you."

As we reflect, we need to take an intentional pause, a deep breath or a moment of silence, to allow ourselves to feel all our emotions. To take it all in. That's where change has a chance to last for more than just a brief moment.

I (Rachel) can imagine myself on the day of my recent wedding. There was so much joy as well as sadness surrounding it. You see, I am what you call a COVID Bride. The person who planned our special day, the *perfect* day, and in turn had to postpone, cancel, change location, contemplate how a mask can be worn with a wedding dress, and even obliterate the guest list from 160 to 13. I had this perfect idea of what our day was going to look like, with all of our friends and family laughing and dancing, but what happened was very different. As I reflect on that day, I grieve not being able to hug and share in this once-in-a-lifetime moment with all the special people in my life. When I stop and pause, I can feel my emotions starting to rise. Greif, sadness, and anger, mixed with joy and love. It can get a bit convoluted and overwhelming at times.

As I sit here at 5:00 a.m., alone, hearing the birds chirping from my patio, I've decided to take an intentional pause, a moment to ground myself, to bring myself to the present so I can process the past. As I give myself to the grounding process by breathing and doing my exercises (shared below), I am able to reflect on the things I am still grieving, but also make space to reflect on the amazing things that happened that day, as well. It's in this moment I can experience the balance I need to integrate all of the memories onto a path forward filled with gratitude and peace.

Grounding is a coping strategy designed to "ground" you in, or immediately contact you with, the present moment." To reflect on the hard stuff, we first need to be able to ground ourselves in the present. That is, after all, where we are, right? Not stuck in the past, but here, experiencing all that life offers us in real time. Grounding essentially gives us a tether, if you will, that pulls us back to safety when reflecting gets too hard or our emotions begin to consume us.

1. Join me in applying the **5-4-3-2-1 Grounding Technique** to whatever situation you need some balance for today.

What are 5 things you can see? Look for small details such as a pattern on the ceiling, the way light reflects off a surface or an object you never noticed.

Take 3 deep breaths.

What are 4 things you can feel? Notice the sensation of clothing on your body, the breeze or the sun on your skin, or the feeling of the chair you are sitting on. Pick up an object and examine its weight, texture, and other physical qualities.

Take 3 deep breaths.

What are 3 things you can hear? Pay attention to the sounds your mind has tuned ,out, such as a ticking clock, distant traffic, or trees blowing in the wind.

Take 3 deep breaths.

What are 2 things you can smell? Try to notice smells in the air around you, like an air freshener or freshly mowed grass. You may also look around for something that has a scent, such as a flower or an unlit candle.

Take 3 deep breaths.

What is one thing you can taste? Carry gum, candy, or small snacks for this step. Pop one in your mouth and focus your attention on the flavors.

Take 3 deep breaths.

2. After experiencing the **5-4-3-2-1 Grounding technique**, how do you feel? (This is a technique that may take some time and practice before you achieve stabilization in your body. Give yourself grace.)

---

3. How can you incorporate this grounding technique into your everyday life?

_____

_____

_____

_____

4. Give yourself a moment to be present. What is something you would like to continue to reflect on? (It can be something that has caused a lot of stress and grief, something small that is making you feel stuck, or even an area you'd like to spend time with God on but the emotion feels overwhelming.)

_____

_____

_____

_____

As we move through life, there will be moments where it can feel overwhelming and maybe even too hard to handle. In these places, we first need to ground ourselves in the moment so we can reflect, allowing ourselves the space to grieve and celebrate, to find balance.

After all, experiencing the presence of God takes place in our present.

Getting stuck in our past or worrying about our future, without a way to ground us where we are right now, robs us of the limitless peace of Christ.

5. Take a moment to read Psalm 16:11 and reflect on what this verse means to you. If desired, rewrite it in your own words as the Holy Spirit leads.

_____

_____

_____

_____

_____

_____

_____

_____

Psalm 16:11

11 You will show me the way of life,
    granting me the joy of your presence
    and the pleasures of living with you forever. (NLT)

Hope

For anyone who has traversed a season of growth and healing, you can identify with me (Teri) when I say that there are moments that can feel hopeless. That all the hard work you've put in has hit an impasse, and all your worst fears begin to set in. What if? What if those moments aren't the end, but rather, the beginning?

When we, as women, begin to journey through Balance, we start to integrate the good with the difficult situations that would have stopped us in our tracks in the past.

Doesn't that sound amazing?

The key is *hope*.

In his group recovery workbook, *The Genesis Process*,[17] Michael Dye outlines a simple, but profound Hope Formula, that I believe will help to serve as a backdrop for us to take monumental steps forward through increasing our self-awareness in our growth journey as women.

HOPE

HOPE comes from CHANGE.
CHANGE comes from RISK.
RISK comes from FAITH.
FAITH gives you the HOPE
To CHANGE and RISK again.

---

17. Dye, Michael, *The Genesis Process*, Double Eagle Industries (2012) 25.

1. When you read this Hope Formula, what phrase stands out to you the most? Why?

_____

_____

2. In your current situation, where do you see yourself in this formula?

_____

_____

3. Where would you like to see yourself in this formula?

_____

_____

4. What is holding you back?

_____

_____

Michael Dye goes on to elaborate regarding the concept of hope emphasizing that, in a season of growth, hope that empowers us onward is more a noun than a verb. "It is something you either have or you don't," he states. Essentially, the difference between seeing hope as a noun or a verb changes the way it is applied in our lives. The verb form states ideas like, "I hope I make the right decision, or I hope I get the job I interviewed for, or I hope it doesn't rain today." It's the nail biting, waiting to see what happens to determine how I am truly feeling, kind of place that we often find ourselves in, if we are honest. Can you relate? I certainly can! The noun form of the word hope, however, gives us the unique opportunity to anchor it solidly in the person of Jesus Christ. The one who never changes, never leaves us, and promises us a future when we seek Him. The anchor holds firm because HE can endure on our behalf.

The tipping point is when we open our lives to the change process that comes from stepping out in faith, and we risk walking the vulnerable path that gives us the ability to look at our current situation, no matter what it is, and Hope echoes back at us that we are resilient enough to meet it, face to face.

Consider this passage:

> I pray that God, the source of hope, will fill you completely with joy and peace because you trust in Him. Then you will overflow with confident hope through the power of the Holy Spirit. Romans 15:13 (NIV)

Can you see the reminder of the potential exchange that takes place when we anchor ourselves to Hope, Himself? We OVERFLOW with CONFIDENT HOPE!

5. How does this perspective of the passage impact you as you read it?

_____

_____

6. On day one of this week, you took the time to write about some realities you are currently facing. How does the truth above impact how you now view your reality?

_____

_____

_____

7. Does it give you courage to RISK or redirect your FAITH? Why or why not? Explain.

_____

_____

_____

The passage in Romans 15:13 beautifully illustrates the Hope Formula. The hope we so desperately desire comes as we confidently walk in the truth of who we were created to be by the Creator, Himself. He ever so lovingly changes and grows us in Him as we take risks in vulnerability with Him and with others who are safe.

8. What will you risk in faith to continue your commitment to growth?

_____

_____

_____

9. Who will hold you accountable?

_____

_____

_____

Day 4

Intimacy

Take a moment to contemplate these beautiful words written by Curt Thompson from the book, *The Soul of Shame*.

> We all are born into the world looking for someone looking for us, and we remain in this mode of searching for the rest of our lives. When we acknowledge our shame, it resonates with the shame carried by all of us. With confession it is given the opportunity for resonance, exposure and healing in the life of the listener as well as the speaker.[18]

1. What are you experiencing when you read this passage?

_____

_____

_____

2. Can you name the feeling?

_____

_____

_____

_____

18. Curt Thompson, *The Soul of Shame: Retelling the Stories We Believe About Ourselves*, InterVarsity Press (2015) 138.

Seasons | Craft · Chaney · Rasa

3. What memory or memories does it invoke?

_____

_____

Intimacy is one of the most confused and misunderstood concepts.

It is a word that carries so many personal interpretations, expectations, and manipulations. Intimacy is a trigger word for deep connection and belonging and, conversely, can also bring up painful memories of betrayal, abuses, or loss. For some who have had healthy attachment stories in their lives, intimacy is a journey of connection that easily unfolds in safe relationships. For some of us, it can be scary, complicated, and ambiguous.

Giving and receiving in intimate connection, both emotional and sexual, are rooted in the way we developed attachment in our early years and beyond. So, what does this mean for us now? As we navigate the concept of Balance in our lives, it is a good exercise to take the time to develop awareness regarding our attachment stories and strategies. Once we get there, it is easier to see how we respond in intimacy with God and others.

Let's begin with a better understanding of "attachment." In her book, *Love and Sex*, Nancy Houston describes it this way:

> Attachment is when we allow ourselves to connect deeply to another person. Anxiety and avoidance are acknowledged and overcome by practicing vulnerability and openness about fears. Help is asked for and sought, when one or both partners find themselves stuck in negative relational patterns. Each take personal responsibility to do his or her own growth work. They avoid the blame game and instead ask themselves the question, 'What is my part in this?' Attachment takes time to build and includes commitment and covenant. To form a secure, solid attachment, people want to know three things: 1) Do you have my back? 2) Can I count on you? 3) Are you there for me? When those three questions are answered, secure attachment can form.[19]

---

19. Nancy Houston, *Love and Sex: A Christian Guide to Healthy Intimacy,* Regnery Publishing, Incorporated, (2018) 192.

To truly live in balance, we as women need to stop long enough to come to terms with where we are, regarding intimacy and attachment. This is true no matter what age or stage we find ourselves in today.

As stated above, when we can connect in vulnerability and safety with others, a secure attachment has the opportunity to form.

For most of us, however, there have been aspects of our journey that, when we are really honest, hinder this exchange to some degree. The beautiful thing about our life with Christ is that He is able to heal and guide us toward repair.

Here are a few concepts to contemplate:

4. Think back upon your earliest memories of attachment with your parents, or what others have told you regarding that time in your life. Was it an environment where secure attachment could be cultivated?

_____

_____

5. What attachment style do you most identify with, and how do you see that impacting your relationships?

a. Secure (Comfortable with intimacy and vulnerability as well as separateness)

b. Avoidant (Connection not a priority, uncomfortable with vulnerability)

c. Anxious (Feel worried, insecure, and needy in relationships)

_____

_____

_____

6. When you think about the significant and intimate relationships in your life, do you experience the following? If so, explain below.

d. Do you have my back?

e. Can I count on you?

f. Are you there for me?

_____

_____

_____

7. If not, what are the barriers?

_____

_____

8. Do you feel you have the capacity to reciprocate the three aspects of attachment stated above to others around you? (If there is resistance to this question, take time to assess why.)

_____

_____

_____

9. Based on these points of contemplation, do you feel you may need additional help, greater understanding, or healing in the areas of attachment and intimacy in your life? What are you curious about?

_____

_____

_____

_____

10. What steps are you willing to take to advocate for yourself and your loved ones?

_____

_____

_____

11. What safe person will you talk to about what you have discovered?

_____

_____

_____

_____

Values

I've heard it said, that *integrity* can be defined by how clearly our values are observed and lived out on a daily basis. Another way to put it is, do you practice what you preach? Do you live your life according to what you believe?

I never really understood the connection between integrity and values until hearing this truth.

Values are important for navigating balance in our lives.

They are our rudder. Can you imagine a ship without a rudder? It would go nowhere and everywhere very fast. The truth is, values keep us going in the direction we want to go as we live more authentic lives. Let's talk a bit more about identifying values.

Often, we initially create a long list of "values" we aspire to, believe in, or wish were ours. The truth is, we will end up with about 4-8 core values that we live by…day in, day out, whether we are aware of them or not. If we live in Balance, we have awareness and commitment to our values being reflected in who we are and who we would like to be. Today, I would like you to think about what your value system TRULY consists of.

You've heard it said, tongue-in-cheek, that you can look at someone's checkbook and determine their values. I'd like you to think about the reality of the things you value, and then think of someone who is really close to you and ask yourself if they would agree. Really drill down what you currently value, not necessarily what you think you should value from someone else's lenses. Here's why; because chances are, your values will change and evolve over time. As you grow, stretch, learn, become healthier and more aware, your values may change. Let's begin, however, with what you believe your values are today.

Take the time to review the list below and write down at least 8-10 values that you currently embody or are working on. The great thing about this exercise is that there are no wrong answers. Here are a few questions to ask yourself that may help in the process as well.

- What is important to me? What do I spend the most time on?
- What makes me feel connected to God and others?

- What lens do I filter decisions through before acting on them?
- Perhaps in the kind of work you enjoy, you might ask yourself, What value do I bring as I do meaningful tasks that I have a passion for, like helping others?
- How important are things like spirituality, family, truth, and authenticity?

Here are a few words that might help you with your thought process:

Achievement/ Accomplishment	Adventure	Affirmation	Authenticity
Art	Beauty	Career	Challenge
Close Relationships	Collaboration/ Creative Partner	Community	Compassion
Conversation	Creativity	Diligence	Democracy/Freedom
Encouragement	Excellence	Excitement	Exploration
Environmental	Faith	Family	Financial Stability
Fulfillment	Fun	Growth	Honesty
Humor	Influence	Integrity	Intellectual Stimulation
Inspiring Others	Leadership	Love	Marriage
Mentoring	Nurturing	Orderliness	Passion
Patience	Peace	Perfection	Persistence

Personal Development	Persistence	Physical Vitality	Productivity
Purity	Quality	Recognition	Respect
Risk-taking	Security	Self-expression	Serving Others
Silence	Solitude	Spiritual Growth	Stability
Success	Trust	Truth	Worship

1. On a separate sheet of paper, list your values. These are attributes and actions you are currently exhibiting and expressing, as well as those you are working on and desire to have. Feel free to add to the list above.

2. Now, narrow that list to your Top Ten values.

_____

_____

_____

_____

_____

3. Share this list with your accountability partner or group. Do they have any feedback for you?

_____

_____

_____

_____

4. Take some time to pray and listen to the Lord's input regarding your values. What is He affirming? What do you sense Him saying to you or guiding you toward?

_____

_____

_____

5. Place these values in front of you consistently for three weeks. When decisions need to be made, filter them through the framework of your values. When you are stuck, refer to your values as a rudder. How are your values playing out on a daily basis?

_____

_____

_____

_____

6. At the end of the three-week timeframe, we encourage you to consider getting really honest while contemplating your values. Review the list you wrote. What changes need to be made in your life to honor the values you chose? Who can you trust to hold you accountable?

_____

_____

_____

_____

_____

_____

_____

Our next growth phase is called Advocacy. Taking the leap from Balance to Advocacy is all about heart. We will be exploring what it really means to serve and lead in our areas of influence, what we need to be authentic in those areas, and what impact and potential our stories, now that they have been integrated and balanced, have in our ability to touch the world around us. This is where we begin to step out of our comfort zones and see our gifts make a real difference.

But, after we've traversed a season of growth, we show up in a new way! Are you ready ladies? Let's dig in!

Week 6

Advocacy Introduction

We conclude the *Seasons* Growth Model with Advocacy. It is no surprise we chose a heart as the symbol of this phase. Let's take a moment and consider what we've been doing these past weeks together. We've opened up our souls' sacred spaces to new depths of understanding and healing. Hasn't it been a journey of the heart? A strengthening as well as an excavation; a season of vulnerability, curiosity, and renewal. But why? Why go through all this blood, sweat, and tears? Because we were created to connect and lead.

We invite you to pause for a moment and take a few deep breaths. What does the concept of leadership mean to you? We'll hazard a guess that the definition for all of us is very different, because it carries with it memory, modeling, and human experience. Isn't it as it should be?

If we traverse long enough through the healing and discipleship of Christ in our lives, we ultimately find ourselves returning to a heart of service and leadership.

How that plays out, though, is as unique as our individual fingerprints. There is no shame here. The fact is, our hearts were made to lead, to advocate, to transcend our own lives and touch another. The how, where, and when we lead is an outpouring of a sacred journey, not just something we sign up for or produce based on our own will.

If we were sitting across from you at this very moment, you would see the depth of passion in our eyes for you. Chances are, somewhere in your life story you were told differently, maybe even shown or forced to believe differently. Maybe those messages communicated that your heart wasn't strong enough, that you were disqualified, or that leading isn't something that girls/women do. Can we all take this moment in time to reclaim what was lost or stolen? Breathe deeply in and out as you ponder that question. If, by God's grace, you were encouraged in a healthy way throughout your life, let this be a time to recommit and strengthen your foundational experience. Either way, this is your moment with the Lord...be curious, be ready.

Self-Care

By now we hope that you are reaping the benefits of a self-care routine. What is working for you? We pray that you are ready to make a lifelong commitment to self-care as part of your healthy lifestyle.

Leadership

Have you taken time lately to ask how people around you view leadership? How do you personally view leadership and advocacy as it relates to you? This foundationally impacts the exchange that takes place in team and collegial environments. If people are following for the wrong reasons, it will reflect in your ability to authentically foster change. These discussions also illuminate hurts, wounds, belief systems, microaggressions, or hidden perceptions that influence the way individuals and teams work on a daily basis.

Advocacy

The Advocacy Phase[20] is highlighted by a woman's ability to take the unique aspects of the previous phases and consolidate them into a confident personal identity. She is able to use her gifts and abilities in a way that is harmonious with her values and goals while, at the same time, impacting those around her. A woman in Advocacy not only owns her story, but is able to serve others through it. There are no false pretenses or shame in the way she conducts her life; honesty and authenticity are the norm. A woman actively growing in the Advocacy Phase will ask for help when needed, understands her limits, and helps others with true empathy, all while maintaining good boundaries. Family and relationships are cherished, honored, and protected in a healthy way. She is able to integrate the good and bad that comes her way, and optimistically looks to the future while being fully present in the here and now. She is able to work alongside and relate to men and women and feels confident in who she is and what she is called to do. Her capacity to reflect upon her growth through the phases allows her to assist and advocate for other women in various places of their own journeys, ultimately leading them with patience and confidence.

Concerning spirituality, a woman thriving in Advocacy is Kingdom-minded. She orders her life in a missional way, demonstrating her true worth and value to the world around her through the unique gifts given to her by Christ. Serving others is an important part of her priorities and values structure, but she also takes time to receive from the Lord on an intimate level. She has a deep capacity to love others, as well as partake of the Lord's peace and joy. Grace is freely received and freely given, yet undergirded by clarity and truth.

It is important to note that a woman will, at different times of her life, recycle through the different phases based upon new situations and circumstances. She will have the opportunity to use her newfound skills

---

20. Research adapted to reflect a Christ-centered focus from Downing, N. E. and Roush, K. L., "From Passive Acceptance to Active Commitment: A Model of Feminist Identity Development for Women," *The Counseling Psychologist,* Vol. 13, No. 4, October 1985.

to traverse and launch into deeper levels of Balance and Advocacy as she gains awareness and resilience. It is also possible that a woman could revert to earlier phases if her current situation or stressors are greater than her capacity or support structure can sustain. The "phasing" ability is primarily determined by her readiness, curiosity, optimism, accountability, and vulnerability.

Thoughts & Notes:

_____

_____

_____

_____

_____

_____

_____

Kingdom-minded

"Some journeys are direct, and some are circuitous;
some are heroic, and some are fearful and muddled.
But every journey, honestly undertaken, stands a chance of taking us
toward the place where our deep gladness meets the world's deep need."[21]

1. What comes to mind when you read that passage?

_____

_____

2. Go back, read it again, and underline the words you connect with the most.

_____

_____

3. Have you taken time to consider the foundation from which you serve? Ponder it for a moment and write your initial thoughts here:

_____

_____

---

21. Parker J. Palmer, *Let Your Life Speak: Listening for the Voice of Vocation,* Jossey-Bass, (1999) 36.

Seasons | Craft · Chaney · Rasa

Many of us have read the Great Commandment and the Great Commission stated by Jesus in the Bible and did our best to respond to Jesus' prompting with what we knew to be true. But have you ever given yourself permission to pause and allow space to ponder who you are in the midst of that response? The truth is, we give from the authenticity of our hearts, no matter what our inner realities might be.

> **I (Teri) learned the hard way that, if we want to live and lead through true advocacy, we must be aware of our internal reality and allow for repair, healing, and growth when needed.**

The Great Commandment reads like this. "The most important commandment is this...'love the Lord your God with all your heart, all your soul, all your mind, and all your strength.' The second is equally important: 'Love your neighbor as yourself.' No other commandment is greater than these." (Mark 12:29-31 NLT)

So, If Jesus incarnate is speaking these words to us, do you think he's taking into consideration the fact that we are humans, and as such, realizes we are not perfect? If this is a possibility, we may want to pause long enough to attune to that, too.

> **The question then is, "What if there is a rupture in our heart, soul, mind or strength that came through an unexpected tragedy, an abusive relationship, a failure, or even a natural disaster?" How could that impact our perspective and perception of God and others?**

Yes, I'm encouraging you to be real here. In no way am I saying that anyone reading this does not want to love God and others in these moments, but real feelings inform our perceptions and influence our actions. (Remember Week 3, Day 4?)

4. Here's a question to consider. What do you do when you are wounded in your "heart, soul, mind, or strength"? Are you tempted to plow forward and forget about what you are struggling with? If you've done that in the past, what was the result?

_____

_____

Have you ever been impacted by an unhealthy leader? I imagine we all have at one time or another. Honestly, they likely didn't start out by determining they wanted to hurt others; most of the time, they just hadn't taken the time to grow, heal, and forgive. They forgot that they are an important part of the Great Commandment. Take a moment and consider if you have any unforgiveness toward a leader in your life. Note the circumstances in your journal, and present the person and your wounding to God trusting Him to heal your heart.

Now let's consider the Great Commission. "Jesus came and told his disciples, 'I have been given all authority in heaven and on earth. Therefore, go and make disciples of all the nations, baptizing them in the name of the Father and the Son and the Holy Spirit. Teach these new disciples to obey all the commands I have given you. And be sure of this: I am with you always, even to the end of the age.'" (Matthew 28:18-19 NLT)

If you read this passage again, you will notice that Jesus encourages us to teach these "new disciples" to obey all the commands He has given us. Hint...the first of these would be The Great Commandment shared above. Can you see how important you are to God and how much He cares about your health, wellness, and relationship with Him, as well as His desire to see you serve and lead others from a healthy place? If we love others as we have allowed ourselves to be loved, through all the ups and downs, we are truly Kingdom movers and shakers! For real!

5. Reflect on the idea that God has woven your unique life and wellbeing into the heart of service and leadership. What does that mean to you?

_____

_____

_____

_____

_____

6. How does that change your approach to serving others and inform your thoughts regarding leadership in all its forms?

_____

_____

_____

_____

7. What commitments to growth and wellbeing will you make to posture yourself to lead well?

_____

_____

_____

_____

8. Who will hold you accountable?

_____

_____

_____

Day 2

Internal Boundaries

In the book *Boundaries For Your Soul,* Allison Cook and Kimberly Miller touch on the topic of the "spirit-led self." They describe how, "your spirit-led self 'holds you together in truth'. From here, you can draw a troubling emotion in closer or ask it to step back, so you can develop perspective."[22] The term "spirit-led self" can look like allowing ourselves to process emotions without judgment, as well as making space for what the Lord is revealing to us. This space allows "ourselves... to have a feeling, an impulse, or a desire, without acting it out". When in this space, we allow ourselves to feel, process, and take charge of ourselves.

The truth is, we cannot lead others until we are able to lead ourselves.

When experiencing our "spirit-led self," we can experience life as it comes. The authors also describe "C" qualities as typifying a person who is walking in "spirit-led leadership." These qualities will be experienced both personally and with others.

- Calmness
- Curiosity
- Confidence
- Creativity

- Clarity
- Compassion
- Courage
- Connectedness

As you have gone through this journey, you have faced the things that you have never thought possible. Now, you have the tools to allow a space within yourself to actually feel without casting blame, allowing yourself to understand where you are in order to create internal boundaries. I (Rachel) used to be in a place where every thought, emotion, or situation I was in would overtake my space. There was no internal boundary to guide me toward peace.

---

22. Allison Cook, Ph.D. and Kimberly Miller, M.Th., LMFT, *Boundaries for Your Soul: How to Turn Your Overwhelming Thoughts and Feelings into Your Greatest Allies*, Thomas Nelson, (2018) 26.

I would feel shame for allowing myself to feel as though I was not good enough, or I would overthink words that were said. I did not have a safe space to go to process those thoughts without shame and judgment. I was ultimately looking for someone to do it for me. But I always came up feeling empty and alone. I was missing the mark because Jesus was wanting to do it WITH me.

As I grew within myself and moved through the different phases, I learned to lean into my "spirit-led self" with the Lord by my side, to experience the qualities of calmness, curiosity, and compassion while dealing with my own personal struggles. That led me consistently to greater courage to be more open and honest in connection with others.

1. What does "spirit-led self" mean to you?

_____

_____

_____

2. Are there any barriers to you feeling confident as a "spirit-led-leader"? If so, what are they?

_____

_____

3. Which of the "C" words listed on the prior page do you feel capable and confident of living out in your personal leadership? Which ones do you struggle with?

_____

_____

4. Where do you think you need more help with internal boundaries in your life? (Example: words I speak, emotions I feel, things I do that I don't want to do...)

_____

_____

_____

5. How do you feel about the idea that we were created to partner with Christ in the leadership of our life?

_____

_____

_____

As we grow within ourselves and move through the different phases we will learn how to listen to our feelings and allow them to inform us regarding what we need to work on personally so we can have stronger connections with others.

To end our study today, reflect on Proverbs 20:5 and what it means for you.

**"The purposes of a person's heart are deep waters,
but one who has insight draws them out."**
(NIV)

Day 3

Calm

When I (Debbie) first heard the concept of "catastrophizing", I thought to myself, Who me? Yes, me! Everything was a crisis; everything was bigger than life or shocking. Even being offended was a life-threatening event!

When we catastrophize, it often shows outwardly as we react in an unhealthy manner and hyperfocus on the ways we've been wronged, or on the injustice of what happened to us at one point or another.

It is often the result of hurt or sadness that comes from trauma or a rupture in a relationship.

Years ago, I did not know the concept of "normal", or the process of learning how to "normalize" my life. When I finally did the hard work around having compassion for myself, and was presented with opportunities to normalize hard things in my process group, I discovered a beautiful sense of calm in my soul and spirit. Prior to that, I didn't have the ability to normalize the circumstances of my life and my reactions to them. I was incapable of experiencing calm to any degree. You see, for years I operated from one extreme to the other, jumping on someone else's crazy train, wiggling into someone else's hula hoop, or being swept away in someone else's tornado. If I wasn't busy being shocked or defensive and becoming highly offended, I was taking on someone else's emotional baggage and making it my own, when it wasn't mine to begin with. Because of my immaturity and absence of healthy emotional boundaries, my actions just made things worse. Eventually, I learned how to become calm by normalizing my situation, which led to more freedom and a greater connection, accountability, and advocacy with others.

1. What do you currently feel overwhelmed by? Are you "catastrophizing" it? Explain.

_____

_____

2. Try to mentally step away for a moment. Is the perceived threat as great as the emotion surrounding it? If the perceived threat is valid, describe it below and list the name of someone you will talk to for support and help.

---

3. If your emotion is NOT in alignment with the actual perceived threat, try giving yourself permission to bring it from "catastrophic" down to "normal". How are you experiencing this exercise?

---

4. Another way to gain balance and calm is by naming what we are experiencing. Have you ever heard the phrase, "Name it to tame it?" It's some powerful truth! The freedom that comes in, breaking us loose from "catastrophizing" thoughts, is an amazing discovery of calm over our lives.

Exercise:

Put your feet flat on the ground and sit up straight. Close your eyes and rub your hands together all the way down to the wrist area. Just feeling the palms of your hands rubbing back and forth when you get triggered, or are engaged in a tense or hard conversation, can calm you down. I have done this multiple times, and it worked wonderfully for me. (Of course, I had my eyes open during the conversation. Ha ha!) It was amazing how much that small act calmed me enough to hear and respond, instead of focusing on what I would say next in a reactionary way or going all the way to catastrophic thinking.

5. List several ways you can put the practice of "calm" into areas where you serve and lead.

*
_____

_____

*
_____

_____

*
_____

_____

*
_____

_____

*
_____

_____

Day 4

Viewpoint

I can remember the day like it was yesterday. It was the summer of 2013. I was taking my daily walk in our neighborhood, listening to music, crying, and trying to figure out what to do with the anger that was deep in my heart. In all honesty, I was trying to outrun it, or divert it, as I usually did. "Maybe I'm not angry at all," I thought. "Maybe it's just passion, or a newfound strength I've been developing," I went on to ponder. Then it hit me like a ton of bricks. Pain, sadness, loneliness, loss, feeling betrayed, abandoned, wholly uncovered, and let down. I had felt it before, it was familiar. I had caught a glimpse of it as a child, and now again from my husband's hurtful choices.

I stopped and took a deep breath, almost perplexed, and thought, "Could it be that I feel angry at God too?" After all, I had been praying so many prayers, and yet, was still suffering. "Has he abandoned me too?" I wondered. "Has he acted like most of the men in my life who have, for one reason or another, made me feel like they were incapable of caring for me the way I truly needed?" I paused for a moment as I looked up at the clouds rolling by and confessed, "God, I'm embarrassed to admit it, but I think I'm mad at men, and maybe you too."

1. After reading the above story, what comes to mind? Have you or someone you know ever felt that way? Explain.

_____

_____

_____

_____

As we women navigate the concepts of the Advocacy Phase, it is important to assess how we feel about others around us.

This means that we need to be open to everything we've processed to this point, and be honest about how others have impacted us, and how that plays out in all areas of our present lives. You see, I have let you into a part of my story that I *could* keep hidden. But honestly, it was a pivotal moment in time for me; and I know that it may help other women come to a place of healing, as well, if I talk about it.

There could be some really painful memories attached to men in your life. I empathize deeply and encourage you to get support and healing if that has anything to do with abuse or mistreatment of any kind. That is what I did. I worked through the awareness once it surfaced. It wasn't easy, but it was worth it. As I took each painful step from Static, to Transition, and over time, began to integrate and feel Balance in my viewpoint, I felt ready to Advocate in a way I never had before in my life. Advocating for, and serving, both men and women feels like such a gift!

2. What are some words that you would use to describe men? (Don't process the question too much, just write down what first comes to your mind.)

_____

_____

_____

3. Now do the same for women. What are some words you would use to describe women?

_____

_____

_____

4. How are these perceptions impacting your current relationships?

_____

_____

_____

5. Did anything come up that surprised you?

_____

_____

6. Write briefly about a time in your life when you felt hurt or abandoned by a male figure. Sit with the memory for a minute. Does it feel too close (overwhelming), too far away (numb), or balanced?

_____

_____

_____

_____

_____

_____

If the question above brought up some memories that need to be processed regarding men in your life, we encourage you to talk with someone about it. Chances are, this perception is impacting the way you are interacting with the men in your life or ministry, whether you recognize it on the surface or not. Ultimately, if left unhealed, this diminishes your capacity to advocate for both men and women.

As I mentioned above, some of the pain and neglect I suffered in life from male relationships impacted how I related to God as well. In the book, *Mending the Soul*, by Steven R. Tracy, this concept is thoroughly explored. The author explains that, "abuse victims tend to respond to God in three different ways, (rejecting, withholding, or cowering), the end result is quite similar: intimacy with God is shattered."[23] He goes on to note, however, that "the estrangement from God that abuse victims experience need not be final."[23]

Take the rest of this devotional time today so sit quietly with the Lord. Close your eyes, and breathe deeply. Let any resistance or walls you sense rising up, fall away. Now take some time to mentally picture you and Jesus together. Do you sense anything that resembles a defense mechanism of rejecting His love, a withholding of your heart and vulnerability, or a cowering in unhealthy fear? Take a few extra minutes to sit in a non-judgmental stance with what you are experiencing. There is no shame here. Do you have words to describe how you are feeling? What do you feel you need in this sacred space with Him? Now just talk with Him. Invite Him to be with you in the places that feel broken and busied. When you're ready, contemplate the passage below. Talk with someone you feel safe with about what you may have uncovered today.

"He heals the brokenhearted and bandages their wounds..."
Psalm 147:3 (NLT)

---

23. Steven R. Tracy, *Mending the Soul: Understanding and Healing Abuse*, Zondervan, (2005) 158.

Serving Through Our Story

We have reached the end of our journey working through *Seasons!* Today we culminate the experience by giving you the opportunity to write a narrative of your story.

It may seem like a strange thing to do, but we have found that writing our life story in third person helps us look from the outside into the deep places at the unique way God has healed us and positioned us to serve through our ups and downs.

It allows us to empathize with the moments of pain we've endured, and the healing that has come...or has begun. This vantage point helps us to recognize that we are human, and we are not perfect. It gives us the chance to feel the range of emotions that are associated with our memories and integrate them toward a healthy overall expression. The truth is, we serve others through our story.

1. Write your life story in third person on a separate sheet of paper, in a journal, or on your computer. Be creative, but also say what you need to say. This is for you. We suggest you attempt to keep it readable, so be mindful of the length. This story is not being posted on social media or published. It is for you to read aloud and empathize with your story. It can also be a powerful tool in a process group for those who are willing to share.

Start with something like this...

There once was a girl named...

Have you ever felt stuck or in need of something new?

Give yourself permission to step into a journey of discovery with someone who can support your goals and needs. Life Unplugged provides numerous opportunities for women to participate in transformational settings, like our Women's Wellness Retreats, that can grow and shape you for a lifetime!

Learn more at www.livelifeunplugged.org

ப LIFE UNPLUGGED

- discover the difference -

We at Life Unplugged know that our strength lies not only in the words we stand by, but most importantly, through the expression of the relationships we live out. We exist to offer faith-based *growth and transformational* opportunities to individuals and couples in need of enrichment, recovery, and change. Our unique change process centers on providing coaching for men, women, and couples through online sessions, intensives, retreats, and ongoing resources. Discover the Difference with Life Unplugged today! It's a proven process that works... There are many options for individuals and couples to choose from nowadays, but what sets the Life Unplugged approach apart is what we call, "the alongsider factor." Simply put, when you dive into online sessions for enrichment or recovery with our certified coaches or participate in one of our Marriage Unplugged Intensives, Women's Wellness Retreats, or Men's Summit Intensives, you will have a trained coach to walk "alongside" you every step of the way.

www.ingramcontent.com/pod-product-compliance
Lightning Source LLC
Chambersburg PA
CBHW082108120626
46553CB00011B/3592